All I Ever Wanted To Be Was A

COWBOY

By Bill Roberts

352-543-5690

All I Ever Wanted to Be Was A Cowboy

Published by Atlantic Publishing Group, Inc.
1405 SW 6th Avenue • Ocala, Florida 34471 • Phone 800-814-1132 • Fax 352-622-1875
Website: www.atlantic-pub.com • Email: sales@atlantic-pub.com
SAN Number: 268-1250

ISBN-13: 978-1-60138-973-2

Cover & Interior Design: Meg Buchner • megadesn@mchsi.com

Printed in the United States

Table of Contents

Foreword 7

Introduction: All I Ever Wanted Was to Be A Cowboy 9

"Deck" the Trick Horse 15

Meeting Jerry Hair 17

Steers in the Canal — Yearlings go for a Swim................... 19

Tom Braddock and the Trip to Lake Okeechobee 23

The Surrency Job 27

Meeting Mr. General Hair... 29

Crate Tucker Cattle at Port Myakka 31

Free at Last — The Plantation at Fort Lauderdale 35

Smokey 39

"Dairy Cow" at Wiles Road... 45

Cows in the Marsh at Wiles Road.................................. 49

The End of the Open Range in the Big Scrub 53

The Reynolds Steer 55

The Eureka Cow 59

Heather Island Bull 61

Double Whammy at the Double F 67

Black Nick and the Rattlesnake 71

Donna Gayle and the Big Black Calf 73

Bad Cows with Bad Horns 77

The Guy Thompson Affair 79

Bonifay 89

Stampede at the Baseline Cow Pen 93

Burnt Island 95

Boggy Creek and the Cement Cadillac 99

Emeralda Island 101

Gary Brown's Bulls 103

Mr. Lykes and the Job That Almost Happened 107

A Trip to Fort Basinger 111

Two Weeks at The River Ranch 115

Cow Truck in the Canal and a Dose of Adrenaline.......... 119

Back to The River Ranch 123

The MacDonald Bull.. 127

Brahma Heifers at Lady Lake.................................... 129

Cow Dogs 133

Buck Fever.. 137

Cow Horses.. 141

Two Weeks at Rattlesnake Island................................ 145

Wild Hogs... 149

Old General... 155

Buster and the Alligator 157

The Barker Gang Shoot Out at Ocklawaha, Florida 159

Foreword

Bill,

Most authors ask a prestigious person to write a forward for their books. You didn't ask, but I'm sending one just in case you don't know another prestigious person.

If you like the music of Jimmy Rodgers, and can appreciate the cowboy humor of Ace Reid, you will love the stories of Bill Roberts in "All I Ever Wanted To Be Was A Cowboy."

At any given time in history you will find a mere handful of men who march to the beat of a Silent Drummer that usually goes unheard or ignored by most of us. They see no value in trading today for tomorrow or being burdened by some abstract notion of what life should be. They follow their heart, and if it's at the expense of their purse, so be it. Bill Roberts is one of those. He's my friend.

Jim Fitch
Acquisition Agent,
Florida Masters Collection

For fifty years, Jimmy Fitch has been one of my best friends, but when you read the story in this book (a trip to Fort Basinger) where I tell about Jimmy turning an airboat over on top of me, you're going to wonder why our friendship lasted so long.

Bill Roberts

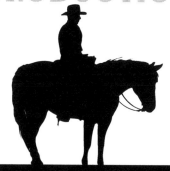

All I Ever Wanted
Was to Be A Cowboy

My name is Bill Roberts, and I'm an 82-year-old cowboy. This is the story of what cow hunting in Florida was like when I started my career at 13 years of age. I worked cattle in 25 counties over a period of 35 years. My only break was a two-year stint in the Navy.

My family came to Florida in 1843 when it was a territory and homesteaded under the Armed Occupation Act in an area that later became Marion County. Where my great-grandfather settled was between the Ocklawaha River and the St. John's River. This area was known as the "Big Scrub" and later became the Ocala National Forest in 1908.

My grandfather, Anderson Roberts, married into the William Holly family from North Carolina. Anderson Roberts and his wife had seven children, including my grandfather, Bill.

During my great-grandfather's lifetime, the settlers in the Big Scrub had hundreds of cattle and while the Civil War was going on, these settlers supplied the Confederacy with some of its beef. Anderson Roberts was in the Army of the South, as were six of the Holly sons. My great-grandfather was imprisoned in Hilton Head Prison during the war, and after the war, he died at age 57, with a mini ball in his neck.

My father married Catherine Dane and they had two boys — my brother, Jerry, and myself.

The first thing I really remember is when I was three-years old and living in Sanford in 1935. There was a house on a creek with a little wooden boat in it that I played with when I could get out of my mother's sight. My father would take me to the tire shop in town where he worked. There was a stone pool with some fish in it. I can still see it to this day!

The next thing that sticks in my mind was when my mother bought me a cowboy outfit, a pair of chaps, a woolly vest, and two pearl-handled six-shooters. From then on, the only thing I wanted to be was a cowboy!

My father and a couple of his brothers had decided to move my grandparents out of the forest where they were born and raised to get them closer to where the boys were working in Orlando. They bought them a nice little house on Cottage Hill Drive, on the west side of Orlando. The first time I visited my grandparents, I was about six years old.

My granddad took me to the back porch and showed me his old cow whip, black slouch hat, and the blowing horn that they used to call the dogs in while on a hunt. On the back porch, there was also a 50-gallon oak barrel with a cheesecloth over the top and a metal dipper hanging by the handle. I later found out that it was moonshine.

When I went back to visit my grandparents, I would hit the ground running right down that breezeway to the back porch, pull the cowhide bottom chair up to where the hat, cow whip, and blowing horn were hanging on a set of deer horns. Then I'd go out in the backyard with the blowing horn around my neck, the black hat on my head, and dragging that whip all over the yard.

Right after Pearl Harbor, my dad got a job on a big farm on Lake Okeechobee. I was 10 years old. We were living on what was called "The Ridge" that was the old shoreline of the lake. After a couple of years, the farmer decided to get into the cow business in a big way. He already had some cows on the farmland behind our house. He bought a 36,000-acre woods pasture that went from Port Myakka to Indiantown on the south side to the St. Lucie Canal. My father took a crew from the farm and built the outside fence around this place. It was 44 miles around it.

Before he bought the place, there was an old Seminole Indian living on the northwest corner. The Indian had built a nice little cabin on an old Indian Mound out of dynamite boxes that he had collected from the digging of the canal. The new owner didn't evict him, but the Indian decided to move to a reservation where he could be with other Indians.

From the time my dad got involved in his boss's big cow operation, I had started in on him to get me a cowboy job. I was just 13 years old, but time was wasting! I was on summer break and my dad was getting tired of me hounding him about my obsession to become a cowboy. I think he thought if I had a taste of the real thing, I would want to be a doctor or a tailor — anything but a cowboy.

The real cowboys on the ranch had just begun getting the screwworms[1] under control on the 36,000 acre C-Bar Ranch. This was 1945[2] and screwworms had been a problem for many years. Screwworms had infected most cattle in Florida at this time and treating the cattle herd was a nasty job. You had to inspect the cattle every day, and on the C-Bar, you had to ride until you found a little bunch of cattle then ride out the ones that were infected and rope them. The doctoring consisted of spraying worm killer on the wound and then treating the wound with a dose of pine tar to keep the flies off.

Well, that was the deal my dad had signed me up for. I moved into the bunkhouse and took meals with the foreman's family. I didn't know it at the time, but the meal I had that first morning was the last one I would take sitting down for a while.

The foreman told me what my role was going to be, mainly to stay out of the way! When they caught a cow, I would bring the medicine. Catching the cow was a lot easier than turning her

---

1 *The female would find an open wound and deposit her eggs. If untreated the open wound would attract even more adult female screwworms and the result could be multiple infestations. If unabated, the process would continue until the animal died with five to ten days. Source: Bushland 1985.*

2 *Prior to 1933, screwworms were unknown in Florida.*

loose. They would always try to hook you with their horns before you got back on your horse.

I ended up staying on the job about a month. I had outlasted everybody's expectations, including my own, when one day, my mother sent my dad to bring me home because, she said, she had some guineas that she couldn't catch and I was the only one that could get them. I was a dead shot with a .22 rifle, and could hit a guinea's eyeball, but I really think it was because she had started missing me.

Well, my screwworm days were over, and I was back on the ridge of the lake (Lake Okeechobee). To be a real cowboy, I knew I had to learn to rope. I had managed to get a pretty good rope, had honed my throw on our two milk cows, but I knew a wild cow was a different ball game. Behind our house was a lane that joined two pastures and in the evening, a group of cows would pass from one field to another. One day when nobody was around but me, I decided to ambush me a cow. I hid behind a tree and waited for a victim. A little while later, a bunch of cows came by.

One little cow about 650 pounds was curious and came over to check me out. I made a lucky throw and caught her around the horns. When she realized she was caught, all hell broke loose! The first thing she tried to do was catch me. This gave me a little slack in the rope, and I was able to wrap the rope around a small tree. It never occurred to me how I was going to get rid of her. She had about eight or ten feet of slack, and when she made a mad dash at me and hit the end of the rope she turned a flip and landed on her side. That was my chance, and I pulled the rope off her horns and ran like hell! She evidently had enough of me, got up, and joined the little bunch that was watching the show. She went on down the lane with them.

I learned two valuable lessons that day. One, not to bite off more than you can chew. And two, if you are going to catch cattle, you need a horse.

"Deck" the Trick Horse

When I mentioned in the episode behind the house on the ridge of Lake Okeechobee that "if you were going to catch cows you were going to need a horse," I didn't know then that good fortune was right around the corner, and, like a lot of things that happened to me during my lifetime, a little luck was involved.

It so happened that one of the cowboys from the C-Bar had a grey stud horse that he needed to board. My daddy told him that I would feed and look after the horse for him, if I could ride him around the house and learn a little about a horse. This was a big concession on my dad's part, because he had always tried to discourage my wanting to be a cowboy. I guess he had seen the determination after I stuck to the screw worm job, up to the time my mama pulled the plug, with the excuse she couldn't get the guinea fowls and fifty other little jobs she had for me. I know

now she was worried about a 13 year old kid tearing around after some wild cows.

Back to the "gift horse"; his name was Deck, and he could do tricks, like count. If you held up a finger and told him to, he would stomp the ground with a forefoot, put up two fingers, and he would stomp twice, and so on and so on. But, the trick I liked best was when he knelt down and let me get on his back. My mother had given me an old throw rug to put on his back, and I'd ride him up and down the ridge.

He was a smart pony and taught me a lot about a horse, and I taught him a lot about fence posts. We would rope every one for half a mile both ways from the house.

Meeting Jerry Hair

After roping the cow behind my house on the ridge (which was the old shoreline of Lake Okeechobee), I was already making plans as to my next adventure, and I decided to be a little more careful. I could see that a career in this profession could be cut short, if you got careless.

The man my dad worked for also had cattle on his muck farm at 20 Mile Bend, which was between Canal Point and West Palm Beach. One day, I was at the farm messing around the shop looking for something – I forgot what now 'cause I was only about 15 years old.

I heard some hollering that was coming from the highway. All a sudden a big steer came tearing into the shop yard with a wild looking cowboy right behind him. To me, this was a magnificent sight. The cowboy made one throw and caught the steer around the horns.

We had a cow pen behind the shop, and we helped the cowboy put the steer in there. The cowboy introduced himself. His name was Jerry Hair, and he had chased the steer from the neighboring ranch, which was the Consolidated Naval Stores' cattle division. They had 10,000 acres of muck pasture just down the road from us.

After meeting Jerry Hair, to me in such a spectacular fashion - I was easily impressed back then – we hit it off right away. He took me over to the Consolidated Ranch where his father was the foreman. He was a nice man, and treated me like a cowboy instead of the dumb kid that I was. He told Jerry the next time the ranch worked some cattle, to give me a job. I just about drove Jerry crazy wanting to know when this was going to happen!

In a couple of weeks, I got the word to show up at the ranch cow pen about six a.m. I believe I got there at five instead. When the crew showed up, Jerry Hair told me we were going to pen some steers and send them to the Belle Glade Livestock Market. He had saddled a big grey gelding from me to ride. The horse's name was "Blue". I didn't fall off or make too big a fool of myself, and, for a while, I felt like a top hand. Mr. Hair continued to work me occasionally. A couple years went by, and I was getting some work with a ranch or two besides the Consolidated outfit.

Hair (left) and Roberts on flooded roadway.

Steers in the Canal— Yearlings go for a Swim

ack on the farm at Twenty-Mile Bend, things had settled down, and I now had about two more years behind me. My father, as usual, was thinking up ways to keep my brother, Jerry, who was 10 by this time, and me busy. We were dreading what he might come up with next, because on a farm there were so many dirty jobs available. I had spent one summer building fence and didn't want to have to do that ever again.

He surprised me this particular fall when he told me he had a job for my brother and me handling cattle. "Great, this is more like it." I said.

My dad had been buying yearling steers at the Belle Glade and Okeechobee market to go on the grass he had planted and that I had spent all summer the last year building a fence around. When he said handling cattle, that was exactly what he meant. He knew the yearling steers didn't know anything about canals and some were going to wind up in them; and my brother and I, with the help of a tractor were going to fish them out.

When you pulled one out of a canal, you had to get him down or hold him until you could get your rope off and when you turned him loose, you needed to point him in the right direction or he would jump back in the canal you just got him out of.

Every time we got a load of yearlings, they'd go on a running jag, and some would wind up in a canal somewhere. We were pulling three or four a day out of the ditches. This is what my dad meant when he told us we'd be handling cattle on our new job!

But we were kinda' enjoying it and got to bragging to the kids where we lived on the ridge of Lake Okeechobee about all the fun we were having and how important we were. Four or five of the kids were bugging us about wanting to help, but only one had a way to get out to the farm. His name was Richard, and we thought it would be fun to see a big yearling run over him, so we told him to meet us at eight o'clock Sunday morning at the farm at Twenty-Mile Bend.

Well, at eight he hadn't shown up yet so we decided to go out in the pasture and start checking the ditches. We were on the third ditch before we found a yearling swimming. We put a rope on him and were getting ready to hook him to the tractor when we heard Richard's Model A Ford coming down the dirt road.

Richard saw us, decided to take a short cut, and headed straight for us. Well, we knew that he didn't know there were two canals between us and him. We started hollering and waving our arms trying to get him to stop, but I guess he thought we wanted him to come faster and he did! Just as he was hitting top speed for a Model A, he suddenly disappeared in a big splash of water and a cloud of smoke.

We had to get a bigger tractor from the shop and pull his Model A out of the canal. It took pulling his old fliver about a mile before we got it started again. He had had enough of pulling cows, went back home, and never bothered us about wanting to help us again.

Tom Braddock and the
Trip to Lake Okeechobee

As I was getting closer to graduation out of Pahokee High School, some pressure was being put on me to decide what I was going to be in this world. The Korean War was heating up and a couple of my hunting and fishing buddies had joined the Navy to keep out of the draft. It was 1950, and I had hoped to get a farming deferment, but the draft board wasn't going for it.

If they'd still had the cavalry, I would have joined up right then, but it looked like it was going to be a lot of marching, so I decided to join the Naval Reserve and hoped to get a boat instead of boots and a rifle.

Well, they left me alone for two years, and I made the most of it by taking every cow job I could find. I often worked the ranch across the road from the Consolidated Naval Stores 10,000-acre steer pasture. The ranch belonged to a cowman named Alton Braddock and his son, Tom, from Ona up by Wauchula, which is just above Arcadia in South Central Florida. Now, the Consolidated Naval Store didn't have anything to do with storing navels or navel oranges or the Navy. They were an old Florida timber company whose main business was turpentine and the by-products of turpentine. Because at one time they'd had thousands of acres of woods, they had stocked scrub cattle to offset the taxes they would have to pay. Hence, the cattle division of the Consolidated Naval Stores.

Well, Alton Braddock and his son, Tom, who had worked me a little bit on their Santa Gertrudis ranch, asked me if I'd go with him to look at some scrub steers he wanted to buy and have them shipped to their home ranch at Ona to put on some good grass. The steers were located up on the north shore of Lake Okeechobee. Tom knew I was familiar with the place because I told him I had seen the ranch several times on my way duck hunting in the marsh that ringed the north end of the lake.

We went up on the appointed day in Tom's pickup truck and met the foreman of the ranch who told us that his cowboys were bringing the steers from down along the lake shore, and he would take us into the area where the cow pen was, and we could get to see the cattle there. This deal hinged on whether Tom liked the stock and wanted to buy them. The foreman told us to wait in the shade, and he went on back to the headquarters. The area was grown up in willows and dog fennel, and you couldn't see 100 feet in any direction.

Well, shortly after the foreman left, we heard some dogs barking and some whips popping, and out of the brush came two steers with a cowboy right behind them. We were sitting off to one side of the cow pen and neither the steers nor the cowboy saw us.

We were surprised to see them go right on by the cow pen and disappear into the thicket.

Well, for the next two hours the scene was pretty much the same. Sometimes it was eight or ten head and two or three cowboys and next it might be 25 or 30 head with eight or ten men on horseback hollering and swearing. But, the results were always the same. They never got a steer inside the wing fence of the cow pen.

A little later, a couple of cowboys rode up on lathered up horses with some hot, panting dogs. Within 30 minutes, I believe the whole crew was under the oak trees with us. One cowboy that was evidently in charge sat down next to us and said they had been hired to do the gathering but hadn't been told how wild these cattle were.

He said they were from Indiantown, and I think he was honest about it when he told us these cattle would have to be trained to respect the dogs and some of them would need to be roped and let the dogs chew them a little. He said if the owner gave him the training

job, he would have the steers penned and ready to transport in a week.

We got in Tom's pickup, went back to the ranch boss, and told him what had happened. This must have been his first foreman's job. We could tell he was a green horn and didn't understand a word we said. We told him to let us know when they had the steers penned. In ten days, he called, and Tom sent up four semi cow trucks and loaded them off to where we waited in Ona. We put them in a big trap for a couple days before we turned them loose in the pasture close to Tom's house.

Tom told me later that on the first day, when the ranch hands on the lake couldn't pen the steers, it was the best thing that could have happened. He got a big discount from the owner who was afraid they'd never be able to handle any cattle on their own. That is, without the help of the one cowboy and his crew from Indiantown.

The Surrency Job

The old man's name was Surrency, and he needed some help working his whole herd of cattle. They needed worming for parasites and spraying for horn flies. He had only one man that worked full-time.

When Jerry asked me to come with him, I was flattered, and I assumed he considered me a cowboy. To my surprise, my dad let me go. He might've said "good riddance" under his breath, but I didn't hear it.

In a couple of days, we were headed up through Okeechobee City and we stopped at the Desert Inn where Highway 60 crosses 441. I always enjoyed spending time there at Yeehaw Junction. There were always some Seminoles in their gaudy outfits and usually a bunch of cowboys drinking coffee or something stronger.

When we left there, we headed east about seven miles toward Vero Beach and turned north on a dirt grade up to the Surrency ranch. There was an old cracker ranch house, a big set of cow pens, a horse barn, and a small bunkhouse. Mr. Surrency came out. He seemed glad to see us, and Jerry introduced me.

He showed us around the horse barn and introduced the horses we would be riding for the next week. After a big country meal that was fixed by a Mexican lady, which I guessed was his regular cook, we headed down to the bunkhouse. I thought I had just gotten to sleep when the old man came in and said, "Breakfast is ready and it will be daylight soon." I was tempted to go somewhere and spend the rest of the night, but I didn't.

Well, we put in a tough week, and we must have penned and worked 500 or 600 head of cattle. This was manual labor and there wasn't much glamour in it at all. But, it was still cowboying, and I wasn't complaining!

Meeting Mr. General Hair

While I was in Navy boot camp, my brother Jerry had taken my place helping the Hairs, a father and son. Mr. Hair was known as General Hair[1]. I don't have any idea why, but I don't think he was a general. I figured it was because he was a "take charge" kind of man. He was the cow foreman of a unit of one of the largest cow outfits in the state.

My brother did have a connection with the Hairs besides working for Mr. Hair. Jerry was dating Mr. Hairs' daughter, Marie, and eventually married her.

When I got out of the Navy in 1954, my brother and I were swapping war stories. I told him not to join anything that the government ran, and he told me never go to the Avon Park Bombing Range. The Consolidated Naval Stores cattle division had this humongous place leased. It ran all the way from Avon Park east to the Kissimmee River, south to Basinger, then back over to Sebring.

---

1 *General Hair may actually had the first name "General" according to the 1900 Federal Census report when General Hair was 8 years old. According to www. lamartin.com/genealogy/parker.htm, the Hair family had a long military history in Florida dating back to 1835. His grandfather served in the Second Seminole War.*

He told me he had never seen a crazier bunch of cows in his life (but he was only 17 at the time). He said you could run an old cow for a mile, and all of the sudden, she would squat in the palmettos and jump up and try to hook your horse. I told him if you were being "bombed" everyday, you would be crazy, too.

Here is a side story to the Bombing range that might explain Mr. Hair's animosity to the place. When the Hairs lived at Micco Bluff, which was on the southeast corner of the bombing range but just across the Kissimmee River, a stray bomb hit their old home place and they had to move to Okeechobee City. I don't know if they were compensated or not, but they probably got something out of it.

I didn't mean to bad-mouth the Navy at the beginning of this story because when I got out of the service at the end of the Korean War, the Navy told me that they would take care of my health for life. I didn't think very much about this until 1989 when I got pancreatic cancer, and they saved my sorry life.

Crate Tucker Cattle
at Port Myakka

I n 1952, I came home from boot camp just in time to get in on a cattle trapping, cattle roping, and cattle shooting deal in a rough pasture south of the St. Lucie Canal. An old cowman had some cattle he had to get off of a leased place. He had decided the easiest way was to sell the cattle in the pasture to my dad and let him worry about how to get them. The way the transaction was to work, it was a good chance for us to make some money.

The owner, Mr. Tucker, and my father would ride through the area and count the cattle they could see and that would be the basis for the payment. My dad and Mr. Tucker knew they would never see all the cattle but this was probably as fair way as any because they both knew we would never be able to catch all the cattle they didn't see.

Well, my dad wasn't born yesterday. In fact, he was born in 1901, and he had learned a few tricks. One of his aces was some reconnaissance he and I had done. We had watched the cattle from a hideout and learned that late in the afternoon they would feed out on an open field that had a fence line across part of it. Next to the fence line, there was a grade with a row of pines down both sides of it. With some hog wire, we could make a trap pen about 100 feet long and about 12 feet wide with big wooden gates at each end.

We made the deal with Mr. Tucker and proceeded to rig our trap. We brought the fence line that was already there over to the grade and left the gates open at both ends of the trap pen. This made a sort of lane for the cattle to walk down.

It took several days for the cows to get used to the new way to get in and out of the field, but it wasn't long before they were traveling through the trap/lane from the field every evening. We counted about 50 plus head that were using this field in any one period of time. We figured we could get our money back from this trap pen if everything went right.

My daddy's other ace-in-the-hole was a cowboy that he had hired. He was one of the Hair boys, Jerry Hair, from Basinger. Jerry was a top-notch roper and woods-savvy. Plus, he had me and my 15-year-old brother, Jerry, which I believe my dad counted as a disadvantage.

My dad decided to run his trap pen idea for all it was worth. We brought six trucks from the farm. They already had racks on the front and sides, and we put on tailgates. We would back the trucks in the ditch next to the grade with the tailgates against the hog wire fence. We cut the wire at the tailgates of each truck so the cows could get into the trucks.

We had to let the trucks sit there for nearly a week before the cattle got used to them but it didn't matter 'cause the farming season was over, and we didn't need them to haul produce.

We estimated each truck would haul a dozen cows. There were a few scrub bulls and some yearlings, and we hoped to get 50 or 60 head the first try.

Well, it was show time. Our plan was to put a man on each end of the trap. When the cattle came in, the man on the front gate would pull the rope that had a weight on it that would shut the gate. As the trap filled up with cows, the back gate would be tripped shut. As the cows milled and started filling the trucks, we had men on the tailgates ready to shut them when the trucks were loaded.

As the big moment approached, we could envision all kinds of problems. We waited out of sight, and as evening was coming, the cattle had made it into the field and were just happy  grazing. They didn't suspect anything. We got our men in place on the gates and the trucks. Then four of us on horseback rode into the far end of the field behind the cattle.

There were a good 70 head in the field, and when they saw all the horses, they vacated the field in record time. They filled that 100-by-12-foot trap pen full and started filling the trucks. The boys on the tailgates were having trouble keeping them from getting too many in the trucks. We had to turn some out of the traps because we had the trucks full.

When my dad and Mr. Tucker first rode through the place, they settled on a hundred head. This was a figure in our favor because there was probably twice that many cattle in the pasture but Mr. Tucker was happy with this count because he didn't think we could get half of them.

Well, we were well-satisfied with this first try, but we knew it wouldn't work very many more times before the cattle would get wise to it. To our surprise, we got two more good hauls of more than a hundred more cattle. Then we fooled one small bunch of about 11 cows and a bull, and this was the end of the trapping. We were starting to make some profit!

Now the roping started. The deal was that everything had to go. It took us a tough week to get everything but two bad scrub bulls that we couldn't get a rope on. My daddy eased out there at day light one morning and solved the problem with his 300 Savage rifle.

Free at Last — The
Plantation at Fort Lauderdale

When my tour of duty in the Navy was up in 1954, I was discharged at Key West, where I had been in a helicopter squadron. I couldn't wait to get out of there, and in the meantime, while I was in the Navy, my father had gone into farming on his own at "Plantation," west of Fort Lauderdale. I knew he was looking forward to putting me on a tractor. I'd had a dose of that at Twenty-Mile Bend, and I had other plans.

I hadn't changed my mind about being a cowboy, but I consented to help him until my brother Jerry graduated high school in 1955, which was about a year away. I was biding my time and checking out possibilities of some local cow work. As had happened to me before, dumb luck was on its way.

One morning, as I was on my way to do some cultivating on a tractor I hated, coming toward me in a cloud of dust was a huge Brahman bull and two cowboys right behind him. Just before he ran over me and my tractor, the men both roped him at the same time and had him stretched out between them.

I got my tractor out of the way, and asked the cowboy that was the closest to me, what were they going to do with him? "We're not sure," he said. "We chased him from our pasture to where he got on your farm. We need something to tie him."

We all three looked around and as far as we could see, there wasn't a tree in sight. It was evident they weren't going to drag this bull anywhere. He almost weighed more than their two horses combined. About that time, my dad drove up in his Jeep pickup. The cowboy that had been doing the talking introduced himself. "I'm Jim Day, sir, and this feller is Gene Couch, and we chased this bull from our ranch where he got out on your farm."

When he said Jim Day, I knew immediately who he was. I had seen him in a couple of rodeos, and knew at one time he was one of the best calf ropers in the state. I asked him when he had switched to roping bulls? He said, "A man has to do what a man has to do." I guess he meant his glory days were over. He was evidently pleased to be recognized, and even my dad had heard of him.

I had heard of Mr. Couch from days working with Jerry Hair (the cowboy from Basinger), and Mr. Couch was no slouch either!

My dad sized up the situation and told Mr. Day that we had an old two-ton flatbed truck that we could bring up close, and they could tie the bull to the back of the bed. Mr. Day was afraid the bull might damage the truck, but my dad told him as long as he didn't eat the seat covers, he couldn't hurt anything.

I went to the shop, got the truck, and they finally tied up the bull to the back of the flat bed.

Well, I could see providence at work here, and while Mr. Day was feeling a little obligated, I asked if they needed any cow help. He hemmed and hawed a little, but Gene Couch reminded him about a roundup that they had coming up and that they definitely could use the help.

That afternoon, they came and got the bull with a big stock trailer, and I made sure they remembered the job offer. I told them I didn't have any gear or a horse and they said that was no problem. "We got more horses and saddles than we got help."

I guess they must have liked the job I did because I worked there off and on for a year. The ranch belonged to Powell Brothers Construction Company, and Jim Day was the foreman there.

Smokey

In 1955, I married Janet Giroux and left the farm at Fort Lauderdale. My dad paid me my part of the proceeds of the operation money that I had put in at the start.

With the money my brother and I pooled together, we leased two sections of pasture on Wiles Road, west of Pompano. A section of land is about one mile square, so this pasture was about two miles square. At that time, Wiles Road was a rock road that ran straight into the Everglades. The land I leased was in the piney woods. The front section was improved with two windmills and good grass. The back section was woods and wiregrass.

The place had about a hundred head of brood cows and five bulls on it. I bought this stock from a local cowman with plans to put another hundred head of cows on the place. The cow people that I had worked for while farming with my dad had always supplied me with a horse, but what I now needed was a horse of my own.

After asking around and watching the want ads, I came across a man in Indiantown that had a 7-year-old gelding that was a trained cow horse. Well, this sounded like what I was looking for. I called the man in Indiantown and told him I wanted to look at the horse. He gave me directions to his place, and we set a time and day when I would be there.

I had a good feeling about this pony, and I pulled my horse trailer with me. When I drove into his yard, I saw a middle-aged man that looked like a cowboy with a lot of miles on him. He was coming out of the barn with the prettiest black horse I had ever seen! He had him saddled and ready for me to try out. I rode him around the yard a little, and he told me to take him out in his pasture, which had some gentle cows in it.

He said to push one out of the bunch. When the cow tried to get back to the other cows, that horse came alive, and it was all I could do to ride him. He was way more horse than I was a cowboy.

Well, I rode him back up to the man and asked him why he would part with a horse like this. He told me his wife was in bad health and he was trying to make money to get by on. I asked him where he got a horse like this? "Well," he said, "It's a long story."

A big cattleman in Okeechobee ordered the horse from one of the best horse ranches in Texas. The horse was to be shipped by train to Okeechobee City depot. In the meantime, the cowman had died, the horse wound up at the station, and nobody showed up to claim him.

The word got around that there was a horse tied to a tree at the depot and some of the cowman's relatives showed up. It was a surprise to them. They didn't have any use for a horse and didn't want to pay a freight bill. A group of people had gathered and the clerk for the railroad decided to auction the animal off for the freight bill.

One of the individuals in the crowd was the man from Indiantown. He was the only one that knew anything about a horse. He was the high bidder, took the horse home, used him a couple of years, and would not dream of parting with him if it hadn't been for his wife's illness. He had already sold most of his cattle.

I asked him if the saddle went, too. He said the saddle, rope, whip, and bridle. I forked over $500, loaded the horse in my trailer, and went back to Wiles Road in Pompano.

The horse turned out to be more than I could have hoped for. He was making me a much better cowhand. You could part cattle, rope calves, or catch bulls off of him.

Well, one day when my wife's sisters Donna and Gayle were visiting, her youngest sister Gayle wanted to ride Smokey. She was 8 or 9 at the time. Donna's boyfriend Ronnie was also there. They had driven over in Ronnie's old beat-up car. After much begging on her part, I saddled him and was leading her and horse around the yard, which was fenced with a gate at the entrance. After a round or two with me leading Smokey, Gayle was getting brave and wanted to ride him on her own.

I knew better, but finally gave in and turned them loose. That was mistake number one.

Mistake number two was not closing the gate to the road. Things were going good to start. Smokey was walking around slowly, but Gayle decided she wanted to go faster and gave Smokey a nudge. Being the responsive cow pony that he was, that was all it took. In two jumps, he was running wide open.

I saw what was going to happen and made a dash for the gate, all the while telling Gayle to pull back on the reins. She had frozen and never pulled back on the bit.

I never made it to the gate, and they were on the rock road headed toward a busy highway about a mile away. Ronnie jumped in his old ragged car and was in a high-speed chase trying to get ahead of the runaway horse. About three-fourths of the way to the highway, he pulled up alongside horse and rider and was going to go ahead and try to block the road, but his car hood flew up and blinded his view. He was afraid he would hit Gayle and Smokey, so he had to stop.

I was following in my pickup and horse trailer, but they were a long way ahead of me. When Smokey got to the highway, he jumped the paved road and headed north. A truck driver had seen the danger and was trying to chase the horse to the side of the road.

Smokey has been running unchecked for five miles now and was beginning to tire out. The trucker finally got him stopped. When I got to where Ronnie had stopped, he jumped in the truck with me, and we hightailed it up to Smokey and Gayle. They had run six or seven miles, and Smokey was lathered with sweat, heaving and shaking all over.

Well, that was the end of my big black gelding. He had busted his wind and never could get into a lope any more. I had to sell him to a man that had a little riding stable at Davie. He was fine for kids to ride because he would never get into more than a walk from then on.

It was a hard lesson that I never forgot, and I never let myself fall in love with a horse again.

Now dogs were different, and I can't help myself when it comes to a good dog.

"Dairy Cow" at Wiles Road

When I was working on Wiles Road, west of Pompano, somebody had told me about a dairy cow sale on the edge of Lake Worth. They said good dairy cows that were springing (fixing to calve) were bringing up to $400 or $500 a head. Well, I happened to have a pretty good scrub cow that would pass for a Guernsey milk cow, and she was springing.

The sale was on a Wednesday, so I decided to pen this cow on Tuesday and take her up to Lake Worth on Wednesday, which wasn't that far north of where I was. Well, she didn't want to drive, and I wound up roping her and dragging her to the cow pen. This didn't help her disposition any. Wednesday morning I put her in my horse trailer and took off for Lake Worth.

The little sale barn was on the outskirts of town, and I pulled up and unloaded her in a pen next to the sale ring. There was a gas station about two blocks away, so to kill some time, I went to the station to get gas and a cold drink. In those days, (1956) gas stations had attendants. They'd wash your windshield, check your oil, and there might be a mechanic on duty.

While I was inside paying for the gas, I heard a racket outside and saw my Guernsey cow acting like the half wild scrub cow that she was.

One of the gas station attendants had seen the cow coming down the road and decided to play "Rexall ranger." He had grabbed a piece of old rope that was lying in the garage and made a hasty loop. Before he got a chance to throw it, the cow knocked him down and headed across the road into a new subdivision where workers were building houses. Well, I thought I had better get busy before somebody got hurt.

I asked the gas station man if he knew anybody around here that had a horse. He said there was a stable about a quarter mile, just west of here. I unhooked the horse trailer, jumped into my pickup, and headed to the stable. There was an old cowboy taking care of the place — a polo arena with several horses in stalls.

I told the man my problem. He said his horses were mostly ex-cow ponies, and he threw a saddle on one nice little bay horse I judged to be 8 or 9 years old. I had brought my lariat with me, and I jumped on the horse and took off in the general direction I thought the cow had headed.

She was easy to follow. There were men in trees, on top of pickups, and hiding in houses that were in various stages of completion. Finally, I saw her chasing a carpenter into a house just as I arrived. She saw me on the horse and here she came.

Well, to make a long story shorter, I got her tied to a tree and went back to the stable with the pony. I asked the old cowboy what I owed him, and he said nothing. He had followed me far enough to see some of the action and that was pay enough.

When I loaded the cow in the trailer and went back to the sale barn, the people that ran the place had the gate to the entrance shut and were waving me on back to where I came from. So, I took my milk cow back to Wiles Road, and in a couple of days, she had the prettiest little bull calf you'd ever seen. That was the end of me and "dairy cows." By now, I was getting a reputation a real cowboy and was picking up jobs with other outfits.

Cows in the Marsh at Wiles Road

All I ever wanted to be was a cowboy. Now I'm 80 years old, and I feel my age. But one time I was a cowboy, a good one, and was told so by many of the cowmen I worked for. Before my 35-year cowboy career was over, I had worked cattle in 25 Florida counties. The type of work I did was called "day working." That meant 90 percent of the time, I was on horseback.

A day worker had his own transportation, his own dogs, horses, and gear. He depended on his reputation and a phone call for his job. A few times in those 35 years, I did work full time, but even then, I always did day work on the weekends.

One of the cowmen I worked for had cattle in nine counties from Levy County north through Marion County, as far south as Polk County, and east to Osceola on Lake Jessup. Also, I was assistant manager on the Fisher Ranch, which was located on the Ocklawaha River between Moss Bluff and Ocklawaha, but even there, the owner let me day work on my own time.

My first paying job was on the 36,000-acre C Bar east of Lake Okeechobee. It was 1945, and I was 13 at the time. I rode all summer helping two real cowboys doctor cattle with screwworms. I was so saddle sore I couldn't sit down for months. From then on, I worked cattle off and on until I went into the Navy in 1953. I did a two-year hitch and then married in 1955.

In 1956, my brother and I leased an old house on two sections of pasture west of Pompano. We bought the cattle that were on the place. A rock road that ran west from State Road 7 into the Everglades bordered it. My wife and new baby boy, Raymond, moved into the house in the spring of '56, but in the fall of that year, we had to move out.

The rain from Hurricane Ethel dumped 12 inches of water on the area, and when I came back to check on the house and the cattle, I found part of my fence on the south border of the ranch had been washed out. About 50 head of cattle had escaped into the saw grass and willow swamp southwest of our place.

We patched the fence, and in a month, when it had dried out some, my brother and I made a recon mission on horseback into the vast area we thought our cattle had escaped into.

We didn't get far before we found out the horses could not stand up in the soft saw grass and willow. We had an old World War II Army Jeep and with some careful maneuvers, we made it to the back of this 10,000 acre lot, which was bordered on the west by a big canal called l-8 and to the south by another pasture fence.

We came up on an old Indian mound that had a big rubber tree on it. Someone had nailed some boards on the tree to make a ladder of sorts. We climbed to the top of the rubber tree that was nearly 60 feet high. We had a good view of a big area, and we spotted a bunch of cattle in the willows about one quarter mile away. We recognized a few of the cattle and a bull or two.

The problem now was how to get the cattle back home. Horses and dogs were useless because they could not stand up. After the storm in 1956, cattle had gone up in value to the point that even if we had to get them one at a time, it would pay to do so.

My dad agreed to let us use one of his tractors. It was a dual-wheel Massey Ferguson, and we put bomber tires on the front. After a trial run, we could navigate the marsh as long as we stayed out of the gator holes. We put a platform on the hydraulic lift in the back, and we were ready to give it a try.

One of us straddled the front of the hood with a rope tied around the chassis like a bull rope. We carried two 35-foot lariats, one to catch the cow and one to rope her feet with. When we showed up on a bunch, we would single out a cow and run her with the tractor in third gear until the cow got tired moving in the soft ground. Then we put the tractor in fourth gear, ran up on her, and roped her.

Then the fun started. She would turn on us, and it got pretty hairy. She would hook the tires and try to catch us until one of us could get out past the end of the rope and get the other rope on her feet. When we got her down, we tied her feet together, backed the tractor to her back, rolled her over onto the board platform, and headed to the house to put her in the cow pen.

By getting out at daylight and spotting the cattle from the rubber tree, we could catch two and sometimes three in a long day. We were making some progress by the end of the winter that year. We had caught 57 head and had gotten most of our stock back. The bulls were an even bigger job, but we caught most of them, too.

By 1957, dad had enough of farming and wanted to go back home to the Ocala National Forest where he and all his folks were born and raised. My brother Jerry and I sold out of Pompano and in 1958 went to help my dad get started in business at Half Moon Lake. I was looking around for a job with cattle, and soon I was working at a Norris Cattle Company feed lot on the Ocklawaha River.

The End of the Open
Range in the Big Scrub

The Martins were an old cracker family that had settled in the Big Scrub not long after the end of the Second Seminole Indian War. Now the "Big Scrub was located between the Ocklawaha and the St. John's, and in 1908, became the Ocala National Forest. It was almost a half a million acres, and up to the time that I worked there, it had been open range.

Now in the late 1950s, it was being closed to grazing cattle, and the locals were having to get their stock out. Most of the cowmen had seen this coming, but I was helping one of the Martins that had waited 'til the deadline.

His name was Maynard, and he had a partner by the name of Reedy Buford, and along with some other cowboys, we were being pushed to round up these cattle. We had penned most of them, but there were probably 50 or 75 head that had gone wild and were having to be roped.

One time in particular that I probably won't forget, I was chasing a big scrub cow in a real rough area of Blackjacks and Live Oaks. I was riding a bob-tailed, part-thoroughbred gelding that didn't have good brakes. He was called Bob on account of his short tail. The old cow had just run under a big Live Oak, and as I swung my loop, I felt the rope jerk out of my hand. I quickly glanced back and saw my rope hung up on an oak limb. I realized I was the length of a rope from disaster! I didn't even have time to kick my heels out of the stirrups! Did I mention I was tied "hard and fast?" Just as I hollered to Bob to "Whoa!" the rope got tight, and Bob and I went down in a big pile. Bob and I were OK, but the cow was long gone by the time Bob and I got going again.

These cattle were wilder than the deer they grazed with, but we finally got most of them out of the Big Scrub. For years afterwards, there were still cattle roaming around, and every once in a while during hunting season some tourist would come in with a cow and swear up and down it was a spiked buck.

The Reynolds Steer

n the late-50s, I was living in the Ocala National Forest in an area between the Ocklawaha and the St. John's rivers. My great-grandfather, Anderson Roberts, homesteaded there when Florida was still a territory. I was working cattle as a day worker, buying and selling a few cows and anything else to make a buck. A couple of the local cowmen, Ray Martin and Billy Holly, told me about a big steer that Mrs. Reynolds wanted to sell.

The lady was up in years, and when I went to talk with her about the steer, I found out she had tried to hire the men that recommended me. After seeing the steer, I could understand why they didn't want any part of him. He was a monster. He weighed about 1400 pounds, and his horns had a good five-foot spread.

I told Mrs. Reynolds I didn't have a horse big enough to handle that big of an animal. She said, "Oh, you don't need a horse, I can get him in the cow pen. He's gentle as a lamb. I raised him myself from a calf."

Well, that sounded like it might work. We settled on a price, and it looked like I might make a week's wages out of the deal if I could get the steer to Swifts in Ocala. At that time, day-working cattle only paid ten dollars a day.

Mrs. Reynolds said she would call me when she got the steer in the pen. When she called a few days later, the steer was in the pen like she promised. I had an old Army Jeep and a single-axle horse trailer. It was going to be a tight fit.

The trailer had a drop-down ramp, and my plan was to rope the steer in the pen. After I backed the trailer up to a little gate and dropped the ramp in the space, it was show time.

The steer was happily munching on the feed Mrs. Reynolds had talked him in the pen with. When I got my rope out of the Jeep and made a big loop, the steer stopped eating and began to get a little nervous. I knew this was going to be a one shot deal, and there was no margin for error.

The pen was about 30 feet long and 20 feet wide. It was made of hog wire about five and a half feet high with a board at the top and one in the middle. That big old steer could look over it anywhere. By then, he started circling the fence, head held high, and I knew he was thinking about jumping out. I was standing a little behind the horse trailer and as ready as I was going to get.

When he came by, I got my rope around those big old horns. This was a surprise to him after being coddled for the last 15 years. Well, I got me a dally (a rope twist) on a post right next to the back of the trailer. When that big steer hit the end of the rope he went straight up in the air and flipped over backwards.

As he was scrambling around trying to get up, I had just enough time to get my rope off the post and run it through an opening by the manger. I brought the slack back and tied off to a fence post and the battle was on. He was pulling backwards with all his might, and every now and then, he would jump forward four or five feet, and I would get some rope back.

Soon, he had his front feet in the trailer, but when he was halfway in, he balked. I had a hot shot in the Jeep, so I tied him off and got the electric prod. When I hit him with the hot shot, he went all the way to the front and almost over the manger and would have, had it not been for the rope through the hole up by the front.

Now I had him in the trailer, almost. That's when I realized he was longer than the trailer, his rear end was at least a foot out of the back of the trailer. Well, we had come this far, so after catching my breath I hit him again with the hot shot and when he lunged forward I brought the ramp up as far as I could and tied the rope around it and the steer's rear end.

Now I had most of him in the trailer.

When I pulled the Jeep and trailer up on the dirt road, the back wheels of the Jeep came off the ground because all the weight was on the back of the trailer. By taking mostly back roads and using the front axle of the Jeep, I finally delivered the steer to the Swift Meat Packing Plant, 18 miles away in Ocala, and I cleared my week's wages.

The Eureka Cow

illy Holly and Ray Martin were two of the old-time cowmen from the Ocala National Forest who also had cattle on leased pastures around Marion County.

In one place, at Eureka, they were having trouble with one old cow that would jump out of the cow pen every time they penned her, mostly over the loading chute just before she got to the truck. They asked me if I would go with them the next time they penned cattle.

I was to bring my pickup with a metal body on the bed that I used to haul my horse and my two dogs, Ring and Buster. They wanted me to stand by just in case the old cow would pull this trick again. When we got a little bunch of cows in the pen and made sure she was one of them, everything was ready.

They had their cow truck backed up to the chute and when they got her separated and started up the ramp, sure enough over the chute she went. When she hit the ground running, Ring and Buster were right in hot pursuit. She got about 50 or 60 yards into the scrub when the dogs downed her.

I rode up on my horse, Shiloh, got my rope on her horns, and we made her climb up in the back of my pickup. Billy and Ray were to bring my horse back to their home place at Moss Bluff.

I tied her in the back of my truck so she couldn't get to the back window and put the dogs in the cab with me.

Eureka was up on the Ocklawaha River, just east of Fort McCoy and the 30-mile trip back was uneventful except that the cow and dogs were trying to stare each other silly.

When we were within a mile of the cow pen at Moss Bluff, somehow she worked the rope loose. The next thing I knew, she's through the back window and her head and front leg are in the cab with us! Did I mention she had bad horns, too?

Well, this suited Ring and Buster just fine. They got to catch her again. But, it was getting too crowded in the cab, so I put the truck in neutral, and when it slowed down a little (I was only going 30 M.P.H. any way), I jumped out and shut the door.

When the truck came to a halt, I grabbed the rope, pulled her back out of the window, and tied her off so she couldn't get back in the cab.

When we made it to the cow pen and got her in, I told Ray and Billy what had happened. For some reason they thought it was funny, until they found out what a new window was going to cost them.

Heather Island Bull

I was day working in Marion County for a group of cattlemen that had cattle in several pastures, including the Ocala National Forest where the cattle more or less roamed over a large area. This was the end of the "open range," as encounters with automobiles were getting more common because of the increase in traffic, especially on Highway 40 from Ocala to the East Coast.

One night a scrub bull was causing a problem on Highway 40. He had almost brought traffic to a halt and refused to get out of the middle of the road. The local law was called, and after the bull put the officer back in his cruiser, the officer decided to call the people that he believed the bull belonged to.

When he got hold of Billy Holly, Billy told him that he would get some help and chase the bull back into the scrub. Billy called Ray Martin, his cattle partner. They decided to call me, and I brought my dog, Ring, to help chase the bull out of the road. When we got to where the bull still had the road blocked, I put the dog on the bull. Ring went right up and caught him by the side of the head. The bull slung him about ten feet through the air, but Ring got up and again took after the bull.

According to the racket, they were heading southwest, but because there were very few roads in that part of the scrub, we had to backtrack to get ahead of the bull. When we finally got to the river road, we came upon my tired and beat up dog. We then knew the bull probably had swam the Ocklawaha River and gone into his old stomping grounds on Heather Island. Four or five other cattlemen including the Martins and the Hollys had cattle in a big area between the Ocklawaha River and the Dead River that separated Heather Island from Marshall Swamp.

About a year later, Billy Holly called and said they had a bunch of cattle in a 20-acre trap next to an old cow pen on Heather Island. The bull that gave us the slip a year ago was with this bunch, and they wanted to get him this time. They'd had him in this cow pen before but he always tore out. This time they had beefed up the pen and wanted me to bring my horse and a couple of dogs.

I brought ol' Ring, who had a score to settle with the bull, and a younger dog, Buster. When they got the bull in the cow pen and had their truck backed up to the loading chute everything was ready, except the bull. About half way up the chute, he jumped over the side and landed back in the 20-acre trap pen. By the time he got up and was underway, Ring and Buster were in hot pursuit.

When he started over the trap fence, Ring and Buster piled him up. Before he could get up and run again, I had a rope around his head. When another cowboy got a rope on him, we put him in my horse trailer. I was told to take him to the Ocala livestock market. It was the day before the sale, and they would keep him in a pen until sale day.

This sounded like a plan. I was to return to Heather Island where they were going to be marking and branding the calves and yearlings that were in the trap.

Well, the next day, I made it to market and backed my trailer up to a gate. At first, I didn't see anyone around, but in a few minutes a young colored boy about 17 years old showed up. We pulled a gate next to the horse trailer, and I told the young man to hold the gate tight against the side of the trailer, and I would turn the bull out — supposedly to run down the chute and into the market. But instead, the bull made a U-turn and decided to catch the boy. He snorted and hit the gate the boy was holding against the trailer. This was too much for the young man, and he turned the gate loose and made a run for it.

The bull was loose and was only one and a half miles from downtown Ocala. I had to catch him no matter what.

I unhooked the trailer from my truck and asked the boy if he could drive a pickup. "Yes, sir," he answered. So I grabbed my rope, jumped in the back, and told him to follow the bull and put me up close enough to rope him. The bull was headed north toward an old railroad overpass.

When we got up to him, he was up on a rise to my left. He came down, rammed the truck, and then came behind the truck. I got a loop on him but with nothing to dally my rope on, I had to turn the rope loose. The bull was dragging my rope and was going under the overpass. When he got on the other side, he turned into a state highway work camp.

I had told my helper to stop and move over, and I took the wheel. When the bull started into the yard, I ran up on the rope with my front tire. It held and even turned the bull a flip. I jumped out, grabbed the rope, and the bull made a run at me.

I had seen a clothesline pole behind me. I ran to it and took a wrap about it, but it was too slick and the bull was pulling me to him. I saw this wasn't going to turn out too good, so I dropped to the ground and covered my ribs with my arms.

The bull was trying to drive me into the ground, and he pushed me up close to the clothesline pole. I saw my chance, and I came up like I was on a pogo stick and landed on the cross bar of the clothesline pole. The bull tried to butt the pole hard enough to knock me off. After three or four butts, he gave up and ran off into a field still dragging the rope.

Now we needed the horse trailer. We had to go back to the market and get it. When we got back to the field, the bull was waiting for us. I eased around on the blind side of the trailer and opened the escape door up front. I opened the tailgate too, and I spotted the end of the rope close to the back of the trailer. When I got out of the back of the trailer, the bull spotted me.

I grabbed the rope and ran back through the trailer with the bull right behind me. I went out the escape door and hollered at my helper to shut the tailgate. We had him in the trailer and soon back at the market.

When I got back to Heather Island, the crew was finishing the branding and asked me if I had trouble with the bull. "No, I didn't have any trouble with the bull," I answered. "Well, how in hell did you get most of your clothes torn off?" They wanted to know.

They wouldn't have believed me, even if I had told them.

Double Whammy at the Double F

When it came time to wean calves from their mothers several things happened. First, you separated the bull calves from the heifers. The bulls were castrated. The calves were marked, branded, and then put together in a separate pasture behind the cow pen.

The cows were turned out into the main pasture, and there were two fences between the calves and their mothers. It took daylight to almost dark and five cowboys to get this job done. As assistant manager of the Double F, it was my job to see the calves and cows stayed apart until they got over being weaned.

I got up early the next morning and went over to the ranch — I lived about a half a mile away. When I got to the cow pens, I saw a bunch of calves headed my way. They had gotten through the first fence and were headed to the next one in stampede mode.

I hurried back to the horse barn to saddle a horse so that I could head the calves off from the cows. There were three horses in the stalls. I picked the one I thought could do the best job, a black Mustang named Nick.

In my haste, I forgot Nick was a little cold-backed, which meant you needed to warm him up a little before you stuck the spurs to him. To make matters worse, I was in a hurry, and I didn't cinch the girth up real tight. I had barely enough time to head the calves off before they went through the next fence and back with their mothers.

I had to spur Nick just to get ahead of the calves. Just as I got the calves turned back, Nick decided he was being mistreated, and he proceeded to buck me off. The saddle, not being tight, didn't help things, and I just looked for a place to land. Nick had thrown me so high that when I hit the ground, I landed on my head. It knocked me a little crazy, but also made me mad at Nick.

The calves had headed back to the cow pen, so I decided I would take the time to teach Nick a lesson. He had run off into the main pasture, and I went back to the horse barn and saddled a little mare. Nick was a big horse, about 950 pounds. Susie, the mare, wasn't over 650 pounds. I took a lariat, jumped on Susie, and took after Nick. He had made a big circle and was headed back to the horse barn.

We were on a clay road and just before we got to the lane, I made a throw. My loop landed on Nick's head but didn't go over his nose. I jerked the rope back with the intention of making another throw, but the loop caught the saddle horn instead.

This was the worst thing that could happen. Nick had a dead pull on us, and I was tied hard and fast to the saddle I was on. Little Susie was getting tired of being pulled, and she decided to sit down in the clay road. When she did, everything happened at once. Nick jerked the saddle I was sitting in out over Susie's head, and I landed in the clay road in front of her. Next thing I know, she is on top of me. It seemed like ten minutes before she got off of me.

I just knew I had broken every bone in my body. I could barely move. The ranch boss got there about that time and wanted to take me the 20 miles to the hospital in Ocala. I said if he'd take me home and come back and take care of the horses, I'd just go to bed. The next day I had changed color. I was now black, blue, and yellow, but I had the satisfaction of "teaching Nick a lesson."

Black Nick and the Rattlesnake

The Double F Ranch was a pretty piece of property with 12 miles on the Ocklawaha River from Moss Bluff to Sharpes Ferry. It had some high ground and a lot of scrub. There were ten or 12 nice little lakes on it.

In 1959, I was working there by the day or when they needed help with their cattle. One time, after we had penned some "dry" cows to sell (cows that don't calve regularly), one old cow jumped the fence into an old watermelon field that was now covered with brush and cactus. The ranch owner, Mr. Fisher, wanted me to get that cow. She had pulled this trick before, and they had had enough of her.

She was standing in the field when I drove there with the pickup and horse trailer. I unloaded Nick, my black mustang. When the cow saw what was going to happen, she took off across the field, but Nick and I were right behind her. I roped her about halfway to the far side of the field that turned to thick woods. In the process of trying to get her to a tree so I could tie her, Nick went crazy. I looked down and saw why — a six-foot rattlesnake was trying his best to strike Nick's legs, and Nick was trying his best to buck me off on top of the snake. I left ten finger nails in the pommel of my saddle, but I wasn't coming off. Every time Nick got back off the snake, the old cow would pull us back on top of it. I finally got my pocketknife out and cut the rope. The cow ran off a little ways and once Nick got away from the snake, I rode him back to the pickup and got my rifle.

I wanted to ride back and kill the snake but Nick made it known I'd have to go by myself. I cautiously eased through the brush and cactus until I spotted the snake still coiled and buzzing those rattles like rocks in a tin can. I shot him full of 22s and dragged him back to the truck. I had to put Nick in the horse trailer before he pulled the fence down that I had tied him to. We told the old cow we would see her at a later date and drove back to headquarters.

When I pulled across the cattle gap going to the cow pen, there was another big rattler just on the edge of the brush. I killed him too and threw him in with the other dead snake in the back of the truck.

This ranch had more rattlesnakes than any place I had ever worked, and I figured it was because there were no wild hogs on the place. They had been killed and trapped out before the Fishers had bought the place.

Wild hogs will clean a place out of rattlesnakes, as the fangs of the snake cannot get through the fat layers of a hog.

Donna Gayle and the Big Black Calf

When we lived on four acres next to the Double F Ranch in Marion County, the kids had to walk from where the school bus let them off at Mrs. Hart's store in Moss Bluff down a dirt road next to a pasture that belonged to the ranch.

My daughter, Donna Gayle, got off of a different bus than the boys, and was alone one day when she saw what she thought was a big black yearling calf crossing the dirt road ahead of her and going through the pasture fence into what we called the Lake Pasture.

When I came home that evening, she told me about this big calf that was getting out and going where it pleased. This story didn't make any sense to me, so I told her to show me where this happened. When we got to where the calf crossed a dirt road, I could see right away it was a hog track and probably a big boar.

On the barbwire, where he had gone through the fence, was a tuft of coarse black hair. After looking around, I spotted several tracks from the same hog. He was making a habit of traveling the same course pretty often and mostly at night.

But the thought of the kids encountering a single boar hog this size made chills run all over me. This was really unusual because I have never heard of any hogs being on this ranch. But one thing I knew, we had to kill him before we had a disaster. I told the kids to wait at Mrs. Hart's store and their mother or I would pick them up until we could catch the hog.

The next day was a Saturday and I called Buddy Fort, who worked cattle with me, and told him to bring a gun and his dog — we were going hog hunting. At the time, neither one of us had a hog dog but maybe we would get lucky and get a shot at the hog.

Well, we tracked the hog down next to the Ocklawaha River and into a big thicket. About that time our two dogs took off barking right into a bunch of palmettos. Buddy and I jumped up on an old tree that had fallen down. All we could see was palmettos shaking.

About that time, our dogs came tearing out of the brush howling and whining like the devil was after them. We never got a look at the hog, but there was no doubt he was in there.

The smell was rank enough to make the hair stand up on the back of your neck, and we knew then we needed some professional help. Once we got back to my house, we called down to Leesburg and got hold of John Newsom, a cowboy friend of mine that I knew had some real hog dogs. John said it would be next weekend before he could make it.

We continued to pick the kids up that week, and John showed up on Saturday with two big Florida cur dogs. We went back into the same area where Buddy and I ran into the hog a week before. It wasn't 20 minutes before John's dogs bayed up.

We eased in close as we could get to the dogs and the hog, and I got a good shot with my 22 Magnum rifle right into his ear. That was all it took. He weighed 350 pounds and had a set of five-inch cutters.

A boar hog jaw has a set of whetters on top and a set of cutters on the bottom. When he is ready to fight, you can hear him popping his jaws together. He'll rub those cutters against the whetters until the cutters are razor-sharp, and you better be ready because he's coming at a speed that's nothing but a blur.

Back in the Everglades on two separate occasions, I killed a hog at the end of my rifle barrel, but they still knocked me down and splattered me with their blood. But I wasn't shooting a 22, I was shooting a 300 Savage that could knock a bull down. And did once or twice.

Bad Cows with Bad Horns

The Double F Ranch at Moss Bluff in Marion County was like about every other ranch I ever worked on; it had one or two bad cows that would go out of their way to hook your pants off. Once we identified them, we made it a practice to tip their horns, so they couldn't do as much damage.

One time while receiving cattle from Dixie County for the Perry Brothers at the Baseline cow pen near Belleview, one of the semi drivers told us to watch out for a little scrub cow and don't turn your back on her. She had killed a horse back in Dixie County.

We noticed how she would get behind a bigger cow and the next thing you know, she would be right on you. Well, we didn't just tip her horns; we cut them off even with her head.

We had one cow on the Double F Ranch that was just as sneaky as the Dixie County horse killer. We didn't fear her enough to cut her horns, but she had put every hand on the ranch on the fence at least once.

One time after we had put the bulls out with the cows, I would go in the pasture in the spring and give the bulls citrus pulp. I had pulled up to three or four bulls that were together and gave them each a little pile of feed. I had walked 20 feet away from my pickup to feed another bull that was with ten or 12 cows.

I only had a little feed left in the feed sack. When I turned back to my pickup, I heard a snort behind me. When I turned around, the little bad cow with the sharp horns was bearing down on me FAST. The only weapon I had was an empty feed sack.

Well, my daddy always told me to use what you had, so I draped the sack over her head, ran for the pickup, and piled in the back just in time before she shook the bag off her head.

You can bet the next time we had her in the cow pen, we tipped those horns!

The Guy Thompson Affair

A couple of years into my cowboying in Marion County, I got a call from a man who was living on Castro Farms, northwest of Ocala on Highway 27. He told me he managed the cattle operation for Bernard Castro, and he had heard that I was day working and had some good dogs. He had a similar arrangement with Castro that I had with the Double F Ranch out at Moss Bluff — we could day work on the side on our own time.

He wanted to know if I would be interested in helping him and a couple more cowboys round up or catch some cows on a big place at Okahumpka that bordered the Sunshine Parkway (now the Florida Turnpike). He also asked me if I knew at least one more cowboy that could help us catch those cattle. He said he had lined up one well-known rodeo clown and a day worker by the name of Burl Stokes, from Bushnell. I told him that I had a young boy that had been helping me and was making a good hand. I agreed to meet him at Okahumpka.

Then he told me his full name was Theo Johns, and he was from Okeechobee County but had been barred from that county for some minor incident where he had almost killed his father-in-law.

I didn't ask any questions at the time. I didn't think the incident disqualified him from the job we had ahead of us.

Theo planned for us to meet at a little country store in Okahumpka, and we could look this place over. We agreed that the next day would work for both of us and a time was set. We both got there at about the same time the next day. I was a little surprised at the looks of Mr. Johns. He had a slight build, 5'10" or 11" maybe, 140 pounds, and showed a lot of Indian blood in his features. I later found out he was at least half Seminole.

We hit it off right away, and I found out he was very well-informed about the people and area where I was raised on Lake Okeechobee, and there was the possibility we were at the little elementary school at Canal Point — on Lake Okeechobee — at the same time.

We got in his four-wheel-drive pickup and found the gate to the pasture. Mr. Thompson had told Theo where the key to the gate was hidden, and we took off down a graded road that made a big loop up along the Parkway. It looked like a pretty rough place, lots of thick hammocks, all over the place.

We spotted a couple of hundred cows, but as soon as they saw us, they vanished. I told Theo these cattle were going to have to be roped, and he got a big smile on his face and said, "Good!"

On our way back to the little store, Theo and I agreed this was going to be a big job. We had seen a little motel over on Highway 27 that didn't seem to be doing a lot of business. So, we each pulled up to the office and asked the lady about renting a double room for a couple weeks. We told her we needed to tie our extra horses overnight to some of the trees in the little wooded area behind the motel. She was very helpful and offered to give us a good rate on the rooms. We told her if we got the job, we would be back.

Now the most important part of the whole deal was the pay. The rodeo clown, Mr. Stokes, had known Mr. Thompson all his life and told us he was tight, but fair, and would keep his word once he had given it. Theo explained to him that most of the cattle would have to be caught at so much a head. From what Mr. Stokes told us, there had already been several attempts made by some of the "Rexall rangers" (or drugstore cowboys), and all that happened was that not one cow was penned, and they had only made the cows crazier.

We figured the negotiations ended up in our favor only if we were as good as we thought we were. I didn't know how good Stokes was, and I was apprehensive when I met him the morning of the big start.

I had a couple of typical cow dogs and Theo had his best dog right out of the Florida cur mold. My protégé, Buddy Fort, had a good little dog that would find a cow in a heartbeat and stay all day. But Burl Stokes had a half dozen little dogs that looked like they were part-Chihuahua. They were tearing around his big old white horse, which looked like it was part mule. I noted his rope on the saddle, and you couldn't use it for a well rope.

Theo noticed the look on my face. He rode over to me and told me because he knew Stokes, not to get concerned. Looks are deceiving. I now know that was true.

Mr. Thompson had brought his regular help, a big old rangy kid, still in his teens. With this noisy and motley crew, we started the big Thompson roundup.

We held the dogs behind our horses as best we could. I half expected the fice dogs to jump a rabbit or whatever fice dogs do. I was surprised how they minded Burl's voice.

We had ridden through a hammock and when we broke out in an open field, there were 30 or 40 scrub cows grazing in this old watermelon field that had been harvested the year before. There was a three-strand barbed wire fence around most of it, with a few holes in it. It looked like we might be able to bunch these cows up.

We sent the dogs ahead and tried to get around the cows. When the dust cleared, the three-strand fence had a whole lot more holes in it, and everybody was chasing a cow. We had a total of four cows tied to trees, and the rest had disappeared.

A couple of dogs had bayed up in a pond, and I was going to check that out. Stokes came by on an angle behind a big scrub bull. As I went to the pond and the dogs, I saw Stokes rope the bull. Now I knew the reason for the big rope. I still hadn't figured out what the fice dogs were for.

I got to the pond just before one of my dogs and Theo's old cur drowned the cow. Well, I got the dogs off, pulled her out of the pond, and tied her to a tree. I could hear Buddy Fort's little jip barking, and I rode that way.

I was riding a big bay gelding, by the name of Mr. Custer. He could pull a lighter stump out of the ground. When I got there, Buddy had a big steer roped that was giving him all he could handle, and we tied on to give him a hand. We got this steer hitched to a couple of scrub oaks and rode off.

Well, before the dew had dried good, we had eight or ten cows tied to trees, and that included a bull and a big steer. Mr. Thompson was furnishing a big stock trailer and a tractor to pull it with. He also sent down a driver from his farm. The tractor was a necessity because a pickup could only travel the grade. It was hopelessly stuck as soon as you pulled off the grade.

By noon when we stopped for lunch, we had about 30 head in the cow pen but we had a long way to go. Mr. Thompson had figured there was close to three hundred head — counting yearling steers and bulls.

The teenage kid that worked for Mr. Thompson was in the thick of things. He was about 17 or 18 years old and he was working for Mr. Thompson because he wanted to be a cowboy. He was riding a big old part-thoroughbred horse that had a tendency to run away every chance he got.

The boy was with me in an area that had thick palmettos and, at one time, had been stumped. The powder company would buy the pine stumps that would harden in the ground and turn into rosin. They would dig out the stumps and leave the holes. The whole area was full of stump holes; some even had some water in them.

Well, this kid had jumped a wild cow, and they were tearing though the palmettos. He made a lucky throw and caught the cow around the horns. He didn't go 30 yards before his horse fell into a stump hole. His rope popped off his saddle horn and when his horse went down, the loop caught his right hand at the wrist. The only thing I can figure out was that he had his hand on the saddle horn, and the hondo of the rope flipped up and got his arm.

Well, as I said, I was with him at the time and saw the whole thing. He had been thrown clear of his horse, but the rope was still around his wrist. He was a big rangy kid and when I got there, he was up and running behind the cow with his right arm straight out.

He was keeping up with the cow pretty good, but before I could rope the cow and help him, he fell into another stump hole. This time the loop came off his wrist. I went on and roped the cow and tied her to a tree. His horse had run all the way to the cow pen. When I got back to the boy, he got up behind me on my horse, and we rode to where his horse was.

Well, that must have satisfied his urge to be a cowboy, because I never saw him again the whole ten days we were cleaning that pasture for Mr. Thompson. The big kid decided he'd had enough. Besides, his right arm was longer that his left one.

Mr. Thompson seemed to be pleased with the progress as the first day was winding down. Theo said there was one other thing he wanted to do. He had seen a little bunch of cows swimming out to an island. He wanted to know if Buddy and I wanted to go with him to catch a couple of them.

Stokes had a long way to get home, and he was getting ready to leave. But the three of us had only a short drive to the motel on Highway 27 where we had the two rooms rented. Well, it sounded like fun, so we took off to where Theo had seen the cows going to the island.

Theo said we would take the dogs up on the horses so as not to make so much splashing and alert the cows that we were coming. When we got to the island, we put the dogs down and told them to go ahead. In about a minute, four big scrub cows came busting out and hit the water heading for the far shore.

It was swimming time for all of us, and it was slowing us down. But, we each picked out a cow and took off in hot pursuit. When we all got our cows caught, we heard the tractor coming and by the time we got the three cows loaded, it was sundown.

As the week progressed, we gathered more than a hundred head of cows, yearling bulls, and steers in the big trap by the cow pen, and nobody been badly hurt yet. The water had gone down a little and was getting muddy around the edge of the ponds.

As Mr. Custer and I were chasing a big white cow around a little hammock, we had to make a sharp turn in one of those slick spots, and Mr. Custer went down on his right side. I had learned a long time ago to sit a little sideways in the saddle in case my horse stepped in a gopher hole and went straight down. I would have a chance to slip off to one side of the horses rear, and he wouldn't catch me in the somersault. It saved me on several occasions from having a horse land on top of me.

This time when Mr. Custer landed on his side, I stayed upright with one foot on the ground. When my horse scrambled back up, I was back in the saddle. We didn't miss a beat and went on and caught that cow.

So, Theo and I were chasing another big scrub cow. I was right behind her, and Theo was off to the side. We were in about a foot of water and, just as I threw my rope, she was on the edge of a flag pond that had a little open water in the middle.

Theo hollered out to me that it was in a gator hole. First, the cow disappeared, then Mr. Custer went down, and I went in ahead of the horse. I went to the bottom and Mr. Custer was on top of me. I was trying to get back to the surface, and the horse hit me on the top of my head with his front hoof.

Things were getting a little serious. I was running out of air and couldn't get out from under the horse. All of a sudden, I was being pulled through the water very fast. My head came up and all I could see was horse, cow, and flag weeds. Theo had just thrown a big loop over all of us, turned his big old horse, and drug us all out onto the bank.

As the weekend approached, we finally got a break. I think we had the cattle confused since we had a lot of their pals in the trap. We had left the gate to the adjoining trap open, and 50 or 60 head had gone into it next to the other cattle. As Mr. Thompson's tractor driver arrived early Friday morning, he slipped around the trap and shut the gate before the cattle could run out.

That weekend we put another hundred head in the pen. We finally had gotten the cattle's attention, and we could drive little bunches to the cow pens each time.

After the first of the week, it was just a cleanup, one cow here, and a couple there, a bull or two. The dogs were paying off now getting right in the thickest places. It was a tough ten days and everybody was happy it was over.

Bonifay

After the Thompson affair at Okahumpka, Theo Johns and I continued to get a lot of work together. He had left the Castro job and settled on a ranch south of Fort McCoy. He was breaking and training a few horses for some cow people and old friends.

Theo had a horse of his own he was trying to sell, and a man was supposed to come by about ten o'clock in the morning. Well, the man was late and Theo had to go and check some water troughs. Theo told his 8–year-old daughter, Gloria, to tell the man, if he showed up, that Theo would be right back.

Theo had no more than gotten out of sight when the man showed up and Gloria told the man to wait. Theo had the horse saddled for the man and the man asked Gloria what kind of horse this was. She told him the horse was all right but he would jab your head in the ground. When Theo got back, the man was long gone.

Theo asked me one day if I wanted to make a trip out to Bonifay in the Panhandle to pick up a couple of horses he was going to break for an old farmer friend of his. He said we would be gone overnight. I decided to go along 'cause I knew I would hear some tales about some wild adventures that had happened to Theo. Maybe I could find out a little bit more about why he had been barred from Okeechobee County.

We headed out early one morning, and Theo was telling me all kinds of stories about catching cows in the Panhandle. When we got almost to Tallahassee, he asked me if I liked oysters. I told him I wasn't crazy about them. He knew a little place where they served them on the half shell. I told him I would watch.

Well, he ordered three dozen on the half shell, and about halfway through the order, he told me to try one. I had almost lost my breakfast by then. He took a big old fat oyster, put it on a Saltine, put a little hot sauce on it, a little tiny bit of horseradish, and some salt.

I had ordered a beer. Theo didn't drink, he was crazy enough without alcohol. Well, he told me to shut my eyes and open my mouth. He shoved it in, and I started chewing. When I got it down I took a big drink of beer. I almost gagged. But, in a few minutes, there was this strange feeling. "Not bad," I said. Three dozen oysters later, I was hooked for life, and I couldn't get enough.

We made it to Bonifay about sundown, and Theo stopped at a little restaurant where everybody knew him. He called the old farmer. It was in January and cold as a well digger's ass. The old man told Theo to come on down to the farm, and they would feed us and put us up for the night.

After a big country supper, the old man started to tell us about this bull that was tearing up everything, and he wanted us to catch him the next morning although the only thing he had to catch him with was two green-broke geldings.

That night, I think it froze everything in three counties. The only warm place in the old two-story house was the kitchen. Theo and I bedded down on blankets on the floor. I didn't get much sleep. All I could think about was that bull killing us and the two horses.

Well, the next morning the ground was frozen. After it warmed up some, Theo put a couple of the old man's saddles on the two geldings. Both horses must have been well bred; they acted like they had some sense.

The bull was out in a little trap pen next to the cow pen. First, we tried to ease the bull up to the cow pen, but he wasn't going for that. Theo took his rope and started to make a loop. He told me to get my rope ready. You could tell that neither horse had a rope slung off their back before.

Theo followed the bull down the fence line, and when he got to the corner, the bull turned around, started pawing the ground. Theo pitched his loop on the bull's horns, and it got hairy in a hurry. Theo's horse shied and started to turn in circles.

I made a quick throw for the bull's feet. I only got one foot, but my horse took off in time to jerk the bull down. When the bull hit the ground, Theo took off toward the little cow pen.

Then, a funny thing happened. The bull got up, went to the cow pen, and just went in. We shut the gate in a hurry. The only thing I could think of was the bull must have been halter broke as a calf.

We loaded the two horses in our trailer and headed back to Fort McCoy. The old man told us he was going to put the bull in his wooden cow rack on the back of his pickup and haul the bull to the sale the next day. We later found out the bull tore out on the way to market, and they wound up having to shoot him.

Stampede at the
Baseline Cow Pen

While working for Juddy Perry, one of the four Perry brothers that I worked cattle for, we were trying to pen 700 part-Braham steers and get the 2-year old steers ready to go to the feed lot at Juddy's place down at Belleview in Marion County. We needed to worm and give these steers their shots before we put them on a heavy ration of feed.

We had spent two aggravating days trying to drive these crazy cattle with horses, and we finally wound up getting them following a feed wagon. We got them in a long trap line leading to another trap down by the big cow pen on Baseline Road.

Juddy's son, Al, was driving the feed wagon and the steers went in the two-acre trap next to the cow pen. There, they started eating the feed we had already filled in several troughs. Now we had 700 crazy steers in a small area.

Buddy Fort, a young cowboy that worked with me, and I had one of the 12-foot gates closed that went across half of the entrance to the trap. Juddy and Earnest, one of his regular helpers, were closing the other gate. Something down by the feed troughs spooked some steers and, in a heartbeat, 700 steers were in full stampede.

Buddy and I had our gate closed and tied up, but we could see it wasn't going to stop them. We jumped the fence just as the steers flattened our gate. Over on Juddy and Earnest's side, they were trying to turn the steers back. Earnest ran over to our side and jumped the fence just in time.

Juddy was on the verge of being trampled, and he made a split second decision that probably saved his life. The steers on his side had broken through the barbwire fence. Juddy grabbed a steer around the neck and rode him through a 12-strand barb wire fence. He landed in a pile of dead and dying steers.

The 700 steers had come out of the trap in less than two minutes.

We jumped into the pile of steers and pulled Mr. Perry out. He was cut in at least one hundred places. Everybody took their T-shirts off and tried to stop the bleeding. We wanted to take him to the hospital, ten miles away in Ocala, but he said to take him home, and he would get doctored there. Most of the barb cuts weren't deep and only a few required stitches.

I still think about that day 53 years ago and how lucky we all were, especially Juddy Perry.

Burnt Island

hile I was day-working in Marion County, I heard of a new outfit that was just getting started in the cow business — that usually meant a lot of work. I had also heard the owner was a Cuban who had been the treasurer under Batista and had gotten out of Cuba ahead of Castro and brought seven million dollars with him.

This gentleman's son was supposedly running the ranch, and he'd hired a part-time cowboy from Mississippi for cattle work. I met this Mississippi cowboy at a little bar in Citra, and he told me the Cuban needed help. I was hired on and worked the place for several months during which time I became friends with this Mississippi cowboy.

When I heard a rumor that an old cowman, Mr. Penner, at Island Grove had some cows he couldn't gather, I decided to go see him. He told me there were about 25 head that would not drive. I asked my Mississippi friend if he was interested in helping me catch these cattle. He said he'd like to experience some real scrub cattle. Mr. Penner told us the cattle were at Lochloosa Lake — in an area called Burnt Island — just east of Cross Creek. He took us over to the area where the cattle were. When it came to catching cattle or trapping them, I'd charge so much a head, depending how hard the job looked or how much help I'd need.

Well, I had never seen a worse place. It was solid scrub with cactus, bamboo, vines, and Spanish bayonets. The only open space was a dirt road that wound around the island and the boggy marsh that surrounded it. I told Mr. Penner it was going to take some time, especially with just two of us doing the catching, and I wasn't sure how tough my Mississippi cowboy was.

Mr. Penner agreed it was a big job and said he would split the price the cows brought as soon as the little market north of Ocala paid us. This sounded like a good deal to me, and Mississippi didn't care, he just wanted to cowboy.

One bright morning, in the fall of 1972, we arrived at Burnt Island with two stock trailers, two dogs, and four of our best horses — a spare apiece. We left the spares tied to one of the horse trailers and took off down the dirt road that wound through the Island.

We hadn't gone far when Ring and Buster bayed up. We worked our way through the scrub to the dogs. They had two cows and a big yearling held in a tight bunch. We got the two cows roped. We decided to catch and tie as many cows as we could and then load them into the stock trailer and take them straight to the butcher house about ten miles south of Citra.

By noon that first day we had seven cows and a couple of yearlings tied to trees. It took the rest of the day to get them loaded and delivered to the butcher at a place called Grinder Church.

Mr. Penner had already told the butcher our arrangement to split the money, and we agreed to wait until we had them all before we got paid. At that time cattle were bringing a good price — $250 to $300 for grown cattle.

At the end of the week we had caught about half of the cattle. A cactus spine had crippled one of the horses, and it was getting harder and harder to find the cattle because we got the easy ones first.

We got after one big old steer, and he jumped the fence and went into another pasture that bordered Orange Lake. We decided to get him later. I got after another cow, and she jumped in the marsh and started swimming across to the mainland with both dogs after her.

I tied my horse to an oak tree, took my rope, and started swimming after the cow and the dogs. About a quarter mile across this marsh I remembered all the stories I had heard about big alligators in Lochloosa Lake. They must have been holed up somewhere else because, thankfully, none showed up.

Just before the cow got to the bank, still dragging two dogs, I got my rope on her. Before she could start running, I tied her to a tree. I called the dogs off, and when I looked back to where my horse was tied, I saw my partner by my horse. He had been watching the whole show.

I hollered to him to bring my horse around, and I would bring the cow to where we could load her. It took us most of the day to get two cows and two yearlings, and we had another torn up horse. I had to bring back my last two horses the next day.

It went better the next day with the exception of the big steer and Mr. Penner said we had done a good job. We had caught a couple more cows than he even knew about, and he told us he had talked to the cowman over on Orange Lake. If we wanted that steer we could have him as a bonus.

This turned out to be a good deal because the steer was in the open, and we had him in less than an hour. But, it took a week to get all the cactus out and vine cuts healed on the horses and dogs.

Boggy Creek
and the Cement Cadillac

The Perry brothers had a 10,000 acre place leased near Kissimmee called the Double LL, and Boggy Creek ran through it. It was owned by a big operator we'll call "Larry."

Well, it was a good pasture with lots of grass and white Dutch clover. We were running probably 500 head of mama cows and the required number of bulls — one for every 25 cows. One day, we were bringing a little bunch of cows back to the cow pen, and I was riding a green mare I was training for one for the Perry brothers. I had dropped back a couple of hundred yards and was putting a little reining and sliding stop on the mare.

Well, she was getting antsy to catch up with the other horses. I busted her out in a run and shut her down in a slide. I was on a thick carpet of clover and her hind feet went out from under her. I came off her rump, but she scrambled up and stampeded to the cow pen with my left foot still caught in the left stirrup.

She didn't know what to think, but she didn't try to kick me. I was sliding along the ground at a high rate of speed, and she was kinda running sideways and looking at me on the ground, as if to say, "What the hell are you doing down there?"

There were several pine stumps between us and the cow pen, and I was hoping I wouldn't hit one. After about a hundred yards, my foot came out of my boot and I eventually hobbled up to the cow pen where my mare was standing. The cowboy I was working the mare for asked me with a straight face, "Just what part of her training was that stunt supposed to be?"

"Larry," the man who owned the Double LL, also had a big cement business in Orlando with several men driving his mixing trucks. Larry was a ladies' man, and one of his drivers suspected him of seeing his wife. So, when the driver went by a little bar and saw Larry's white convertible Cadillac, he stopped, eased up, and looked in the bar.

Sure enough, Larry and the driver's wife were cuddled up in a booth. So, he just eased back into his cement truck — which was still mixing cement — pulled it up to Larry's Cadillac and filled it up to the brim with cement.

I couldn't help but wonder after hearing that tale, "Did that put a stop to Larry's womanizing days?"

Emeralda Island

This area with the pretty name is northeast of Leesburg. Lake Griffin borders it on the west, and Haines Creek is on the south side. You can enter it from the northeast across a fill grade through a marsh and leave at Lisbon. It's a real fertile place with several farms and ranches and some rough hammocks on it.

I had worked cattle on it several times for different ranches, but one time in particular stands out. Theo Johns, John Newsom, and three or four other cowboys, including me, had got the job of getting 18 or 20 Brahman steers. The steers belonged to a man who had lost his lease, and they couldn't be penned. They had been run with four-wheelers until they were crazy.

On our second day, we had six or seven left to catch. Theo had seen one big steer run into a thick area that had gallberries and dog fennel higher than a man's head. Theo and I decided to tie our horses on the edge of the thicket and work our way through to the steer and run him out. At the time, the dogs were with John Newson. When we came up on the steer, he was lying down, and we were almost on top of him before we saw him. That's when it dawned on us we were in a bad situation. We both grabbed a hand full of dog fennel and tried to hide. The steer ran right up to us, blew snot all over us, and kept on going!

We ran back to our horses and took off after him. He was headed to a palm hammock, and just as he got there, I roped him. I had to make a big loop just to get my rope over those big horns and I "yoked" him, which means my loop came down around his chest instead of his horns. He had a dead pull on my horse. He outweighed us by a couple hundred pounds, and down we went. He was pulling us along the ground, but we finally lodged behind a palm tree just as Theo got a rope on him.

My little sorrel gelding didn't seem the worst for wear, and we had worked ourselves out of a job once again.

Gary Brown's Bulls

ary Brown from Webster called me one night in the late 1960s and said that he had heard that I had some good dogs that could catch anything on four feet. He told me about his rough pasture south of Center Hill that they had gathered everything out of, except for four mean Hereford-cross bulls that wouldn't go. The fifth had jumped the fence before we got there, and they had shot him! He said they were about as mean a bunch as he had ever seen.

We set a date, and I got three good dogs and one other cowboy to help me. When we made a round by the edge of a pond, we saw three of the bulls across the marsh about a quarter mile away. We took off after the biggest bull and got him roped at the edge of a thick hammock. We tied him to a tree and took off through the woods after another bull.

We got separated in the hammock, and I came up on a single bull hiding in palmettos. I got him roped and was about to tie him to an oak tree when I saw a big hornet nest hanging in the tree. So far, the hornets weren't upset, so I pulled the bull away quietly and found another tree to hitch him to. This was too close to disaster, and I had broken out in a cold sweat.

The other cowboy, Buddy Fort, was out of the hammock and into an open prairie. I was feeling lucky about the hornet deal when, all of a sudden, a bull came out of the palmettos where he had been hiding. Before my horse Shiloh could react, the bull hit him in the shoulder. I took my left foot out of the stirrup and tried to shove the bull away from Shiloh, but the left horn of the bull went through the stirrup.

My horse was heading west and the bull was heading east. When the horn popped out of the stirrup, it spun Shiloh 180-degrees. This made him as mad as a wet hen. Before I could get orientated, Shiloh was right on the bull's tail with his ears laid back, and all I had to do was put the loop on the bull.

I now had caught two bulls by myself, and we had another one between us. So, that left one.

As we were to discover, he was not the biggest, but he was the baddest of the bunch. The dogs had him bayed up in a thicket of cat claw vines and scrub oak. There was no room to swing a rope, and the dogs had been whipped. They had caught the bull but he had slung them off.

We finally hit on a plan. I climbed the oak tree he was under. We had tied our two ropes together. Buddy had one end, and I had the end with the loop. I managed to get the rope around the bull's horns, and Buddy pulled him out of the bushes and vines. When he was in the open, the dogs got some of their courage back and covered him up head to tail.

It was about one o'clock, and it took the rest of the afternoon to put the bulls into the horse trailer — one at a time — and transport them to the cow pen at Gary Brown's main place.

You can believe we took special care getting that one bull away from the hornet's nest.

Mr. Lykes and the Job That Almost Happened

Normally, I would not talk about the many deals that fell through on us, but I'd like to share with you what happened on this "almost job" and what my partner and I learned on this trip to Lykes Brothers at Brighton.

In the early 70s, Theo Johns and I were winding down a project at McIntosh where we were catching some Angus cattle for a little cow and horse ranching outfit that was going broke. They had 75 or 80 Angus cows that they had to get rid of, and they had no idea how to get these cattle that they had spoiled and couldn't even get close to.

Well, we got most of them, and we had worked ourselves out of a job and no prospect in sight for anything else when we heard a rumor about some action in Okeechobee County.

The Lykes Brothers were taking bids to catch some 14-year-old steers they had marked and branded as yearlings and hadn't seen much of since. They had trapped a few in the last 14 years, but not all. There were close to a hundred left, and they wanted them caught but didn't have the help or the time to do it themselves.

Big steers in the thousand pound range were bringing good money at slaughter at this time, and they figured they could pay some professional cowboys to catch them and still make a profit.

Theo called down to Brighton and talked to Charley Lykes himself. He was interested and wanted us to come down and talk to him about the job. We set a date to go down and got there early on a Monday.

Mr. Lykes was an interesting man and treated us well. He wanted to know about our experience, and we gave him several references. He said he would check them out.

Theo was keeping a low profile in Okeechobee County as he had been barred from the county — something to do with an incident that happened many years ago. We were hoping the statute of limitations had run out on this. Mr. Lykes said he could put us up in their bunkhouse. We spent the night on the ranch. The next day, we were to get with his foreman, and he would take us around the area that the steers were supposed to be in.

When we got to the headquarters the next morning, Mr. Lykes called us in his office. He showed us a big mounted steer head on the wall and said this was what they looked like. He said they shot this old steer and had his head mounted. His horns must have been six feet apart from tip to tip. I told Theo we'd have to get longer ropes.

Well, that morning we loaded up with his foreman into the pickup and took off to the area where the steers were last seen. It must have been nearly noon before we saw the first steer, but we had seen deer, turkey, and wild hogs aplenty.

As we came around a little hammock, three monster-sized steers tore out of the thicket and, in a couple seconds, had completely disappeared. They were every color of the rainbow, and all had big horns. The rest of the day we probably saw eight or ten more, and the foreman told us he had spent a lot of time trying to estimate how many were left and allowing for the age, he put the number to about 70 or 80 head.

All this time, Theo and I were calculating the amount of horses and dogs and time it would take to hunt and catch these wild cattle, and when we got back to Mr. Lykes, we gave him a price. We told him that for us to travel from Marion County and bring our horses and dogs and it might take 10 days or two weeks to get them all. We would need a least $80 a head. He wrote this down and told us he would let us know.

We had heard that Lykes was always cheap and after staying in their bunkhouse and meeting his cowboys and seeing their gear, we believed it. They used croaker bags for saddle blankets and some still rode McClellan saddles.

In about a week, we heard through the cowboy wireless (or the rumor mill) that some local Okeechobee boys had got the job at $35 a head. On their last day on the job had got a high-priced stud horse killed by a big old rig (a bull with one testicle), and they wound up shooting the old (almost) steer.

Theo and I both took a sigh of relief and knew we had dodged a bullet.

A Trip to Fort Basinger

had a good friend, Jimmy Fitch, who was living on the old site of Fort Basinger from the Seminole Wars. It was on the west side of the Kissimmee River. I said Jimmy was a good friend but only if you call somebody that nearly killed you, "a good friend."

Back in the 50s, Jimmy and I were in his airboat west of Andytown, in the Everglades. We had jumped a little buck deer, and we were chasing him just to give him a little scare. We didn't want to hurt him.

We hit a tussock with the airboat as we were making a turn. The airboat flipped up on its side, and I went overboard. Jimmy kept his cool and powered the boat in a circle around me. In those days, we didn't know what a prop guard was, so I got down in the water as far as I could, but it was only two feet deep.

All I could see was that big yellow prop spinning about a foot from my head. But, Jimmy kept the power on and the boat eventually came back down flat. He shut the motor off; I got in and told Jimmy, "Let's go home. I've had about all the fun I can stand for one day."

Well, all of this was water under the bridge and about ten years later, I had endeared myself to Jimmy and his wife, Ann, although maybe it should have been the other way around.

Jimmy and Anne's boys were in the Future Farmers of America and were going to show some steers at a big livestock event in Sebring. Jimmy knew that I had contacts with several cattlemen in Marion County that raised some outstanding calves. I knew a man in Weirsdale that had some Charolais-cross calves that I felt would do a good job for Jimmy's boys. The cattleman that Jimmy got the two winners from was Frank Smith of Summerfield then and Weirsdale now.

One of the steers turned out to be a Grand Champion of the show and another was the reserve Champion, and after that, I was a hero to the whole Fitch family.

Around Marion County in the 60s, where I was day-working cattle for several cow outfits, the work was getting scarce. It was probably due to all the new subdivisions being developed and the fact that most of the cattlemen leased their pastures from speculators.

There had been a building boom in Central Florida for several years, but I'll have to admit I was missing the wide-open prairies of Okeechobee County, where I was raised and began my cowboy days.

So, I called Jimmy and told him I was coming down to look for work on a big ranch, and he insisted I stay with him and Ann. I showed up with my pickup, horse trailer, and one of my best horses. They put me up and stalled the horse in their barn.

The next day, Jimmy took me over to the Griffin Ranch on Eagle Island Road. The foreman there told me the ranch was in the process of being leased to a big cowman from Marion County, Jackie Cullison, who happened to be a friend of mine.

I didn't pick up a job, but before I left for home, since Jimmy wasn't a cowboy, he asked me if I could get one of his cows back that had got out and was roaming around in some woods nearby. I located her, roped her, and dragged her home. I guess I owed him.

I went back to Marion County, got with Jackie Cullison, and he offered me a job back at the Griffin ranch down near Jimmy's at Fort Basinger.

Two Weeks at The River Ranch

On a little trip to South Florida, I had done some checking around with some ranchers in Okeechobee. I was staying with a friend of mine on the Kissimmee River at Basinger. He took me to a big ranch called The River Ranch that was owned by a Mr. Griffen and introduced me to the foreman.

After talking awhile to Mr. Crews, he told me that it looked like the ranch was going to change hands and some big shot from the Ocala area was going to buy the cattle. Well, I didn't give that a whole lot of thought, and he never mentioned any names.

So, about five or six months later, I was back in Marion County, and I was approached by Jackie Cullison. He was a big operator in that area with a lot of cattle. He had married into some money and was expanding his operation.

He wanted to know if I would make a trip back to Okeechobee with him for a couple of weeks and help him gather the cattle that he had bought at The River Ranch. So, I agreed to do that and I took a local cowboy, Buddy Fort, with me.

He was a boy that had been day-working with me for a long time, and he wanted to see some different territory. We both went down to The River Ranch and settled down in one of the bunkhouses. Jackie had hired another friend of mine out of Ocala to ramrod the outfit.

It turned out to be Charlie McKnight who I had day-worked for quite a bit, but at the time I knew Charlie, he was a happy-go-lucky fellow, and it seemed to me like he didn't really care if he got involved in a lot of work or not. But anyway, he was the foreman, so I had to do what he said.

In a couple of days, we began to organize the trip to gather the cattle off The River Ranch. Down on the Kissimmee River, a lot of those cattle would come and go to the islands in the river. Some of them would swim out, but they could wade out to most places.

We had to get those cattle off of the islands first. Charlie hired a couple of airboats, and we gathered up our crew at a place called

Micco Bluff, which was on the southwest corner of The River Ranch.

The River Ranch was a big place. It was a hundred sections, 100 square miles, 640 acres to a section. Once we got our crew in there (I think there were probably eight of us), the airboats ran the cattle off the islands, and we would pick up that bunch of cattle.

We had to gather all the cattle in the pastures as we went. The pastures were a mile wide and five miles long. So, we had to ride five miles to the far end, bring the cattle that we found up there — most times in little bunches — bring them back down to the line fence, and put them into the next fenced in area, which was another mile wide and five miles long.

There were five of these before we could get to a cow pen. It would take the whole day to clean one of these pastures. The first pasture didn't have that many cattle, mostly what we brought off the river. We had 200 or 300 head of them.

Then, we would put them in the next trap, and the next day after cooking on the trail and camping along the line fence, we would clean the next pasture. And so on and so on as we made it to the cow pen at the Peavine Trail.

The trail was the old original road — if you could call it a road. It was more than just a trail because a lot of cattle had traveled over it. It was the way the settlers had come into the Okeechobee area a hundred years before. The trail was well defined. It ran the whole length of The River Ranch, probably a good ten miles or more through the ranch.

There was a big cow pen there, and we managed to get our cattle situated like we wanted them. We sold some steers and sent them to the cow sale in Okeechobee City. We had about five semis come in and load the steers. In two or three loads apiece, they probably took more than 300 head to the sale.

That left us with 800 or 900 head that we had to take to the main ranch headquarters, and it was a good five miles away. The headquarters was set in the middle of the ranch, and there was another ten miles on the other side of it. Like I said, it was a big place, and it ran way up north all the way to the Maxie pasture.

The two weeks I was there I never got to see much of the place but we were working mainly in cattle that had been grouped in little bunches to make it easier for us to count and buy them.

Cow Truck in the Canal and a Dose of Adrenaline

ack in the late 1960s, I left Marion County and went back to Okeechobee County. I took my wife, Jan, and three kids, Ray, Paul, and Donna Gayle, and moved into a house on the 20,000-acre Rollins Ranch at Fort Drum. At the time, I had two good horses. One of them was a bay cutting horse that was well on its way. I had been invited to a neighboring ranch, The River Ranch, to work the bay horse, and I wanted to go show him off. It was a Sunday morning in the spring of 1968.

My oldest boy, Ray, was going with me in our two-ton cow truck. The horse was at the main cow pen, and we were going to pick him up on the way. To get to the cow pen, I had to go along a farm road next to a canal. It had rained hard the night before, and as I drove around a big mud puddle next to the drainage canal, the bank next to the canal suddenly caved in, and the truck went in on the right side.

It was like slow motion, and Ray tried to go out the passenger door. When the truck hit the bottom of the canal, Ray was pinned in by the door. All I could see where Ray had been was bubbles.

I dove down and got a hold of him but couldn't budge him. I knew he didn't have much time, so I got his head in both hands and forced it up just out of the water, so that he could get a breath of air. Then I went back down to see what had him stuck. His shoulder was caught in the passenger door.

I came back up, grabbed the steering wheel with my left hand, reached down around him just under his right arm, and pulled with all my might. He popped up, and we both climbed out the driver's side window.

It was then that I remembered that Buster was in the dog box on the down side of the truck. I left Ray spitting up canal water. Before I dove down, I could see that the truck had come up a little bit in the canal, and Buster had his nose stuck up through the grate of the dog box.

I knew Buster was getting air, but I also knew I had to get him out of there. So, I went down underneath the dog box and opened the door. I tried to drag him out but his front feet were wedged in the grate, and I couldn't budge him.

When I came back up, I noticed that the truck had raised at least six inches and Buster was getting plenty of air. I went back around, and Ray was sitting on the ground and was in pretty good shape. He was breathing good and evidently hadn't swallowed that much water. I was only about 100 yards past a repair shop, and I ran back down there hoping to find someone, but it was a Sunday and no one was there. A couple of big tractors were sitting there, and I found one with a key in one of them. I also found a big chain on the shop floor.

I drove the tractor back down to the canal, hooked the chain onto the top of the body, and the tractor pretty much pulled the truck out of the water. I left the tractor in gear to hold the truck up. I went back down and got a hold of Buster, and I was able to get him out of there. He was breathing OK.

I ran back down to the shop and found a phone there. I called over to The River Ranch and told the people there what had happened to us. They were wondering why I hadn't shown up. They brought a tractor down from the ranch, and we managed to get the truck back up on the road. I had insurance on the truck, so I wasn't all that worried about it.

I called a garage in Okeechobee City on Monday morning. I gave them my insurance information, and they said they would send a wrecker out to pick up the truck. They called me in about a week when they had it running — they changed the oil and all that stuff. So, I went to get the truck.

When I climbed into the cab, I noticed that the steering wheel was bent at about a 30-degree angle toward the passenger side of the truck. I asked the shop manager if he knew what happened. He said it was like that when we brought it in but couldn't figure out what happened to it.

I got to thinking later. There was only one way that steering wheel could have gotten bent. It was what I call an adrenaline rush when I was reaching around to grab Ray and was using the steering wheel for leverage to pull him free of the door.

The rush came on from being half scared to death that my boy was going to drown. By the way, I drove that truck with the bent steering wheel for quite awhile before I got rid of it.

Back to The River Ranch

About a year after my two weeks at The River Ranch, I was working at the neighboring Rollins Ranch, the outfit where I baptized my cow truck, my dog, and my son Ray.

Rollins' management wanted to buy some good heifers to replace some of their brood cows that were getting old. I told the foreman that I had worked a couple hundred head of crossbred heifers when I was at The River Ranch a year ago, and I knew Jackie Cullison wanted to sell some of his cattle.

I told the foreman at Rollins that I'd call Charlie McKnight at The River Ranch and see if they still had the crossbred heifers for sale. Charlie told me about 150 heifers were left, and after looking at them, the manager from Rollins made a deal.

We sent a crew to help drive the heifers the ten miles across The River Ranch and another five miles to Rollins cow pen, where we would mark and brand them with the Rollins brand.

When we left The River Ranch with the heifers, they wanted to run and give us a lot of trouble trying to hold them together, but we had good dogs. We roped and drug a half of dozen cows back to the herd and, after a couple of miles, had them under control.

While we were driving the heifers to Rollins Ranch, Charlie McKnight, who was the ramrod of The River Ranch for Jackie Cullison, asked me if I would come to work for them. It was about time for a change of scenery, as I'd had an experience with a couple of the cowboys that had led me to not trust them. The foreman of Rollins told me about a big old outlaw cow that they couldn't get out of the woods, in a pasture across US 441. She had been there for a year all by herself. He told me one of the owners had told him he could have her if he could catch her. He asked me if I thought my dog Buster could find her. I told him if she was still there, Buster would find her. I asked them what they wanted to do with her when we got her because I knew where we could sell the cow. I had worked on a couple ranches in Orlando and had met some people at a little slaughterhouse south of Orlando.

This sounded like a plan — if we could catch the cow. We took my dun gelding Shiloh and Buster and went across Hwy 441 to where the cow supposedly was. We turned Buster out and told him to find the cow. All Buster needed was to be turned loose and in about 30 minutes, we heard him bay up.

I rode to the sound, and Buster had caught her by the ear. I got a rope on her. The boys brought the truck and trailer. We loaded her in the trailer, which had a partition, so we could also put Shiloh in next to her. We took the horse and Buster back to the ranch and took off for Orlando.

We took the cow to the slaughterhouse and sold her. They wanted to give us a check, but we needed cash so we gave them a discount and got most of it in cash.

They wanted to go to a topless place in Orlando. We spent some time at one of the topless places and decided we had better head back to Ft. Drum, where we lived on the Rollins ranch. I had sent my wife and kids back to Marion County because the work here had almost run out. One of the cowboys with us, Jimmy, wanted to make one stop in a place on the edge of Orlando. The place looked pretty scary to both me and the other cowboy, who was the foreman of Rollins, and we stayed in the truck. When Jimmy came out of the place, he was popping a handful of little green pills. He was acting crazy by the time we finished the 70-mile drive back.

I had barely settled down in bed when I got a frantic phone call from Jimmy's wife. She said Jimmy had a gun and was going to kill her. When I got next door, the foreman who lived in the third house was already there and was trying to calm Jimmy.

We sat on each side of Jimmy on the couch. He had a shotgun between his legs and indicated he was going to shoot us, too. We decided we had better grab him and take the gun away. After quite a fight, we got the gun and gave it to his wife to hide.

In the meantime, his wife had called the sheriff's office in Okeechobee City. We knew we could not turn Jimmy loose because he had other guns in his bedroom, but he had settled down and said he was sorry. He said he was OK, and he just wanted a drink.

Well, he fooled us, and we let him loose. He said that he would just get a bottle and everyone would have a drink. He went behind the bar, brought a big whiskey bottle out, broke the big end off, and said, "I'm going to cut you two bastards."

About that time, the deputy from the sheriff's department walked in. He knew Jimmy from a couple of times he had to haul him to the sheriff's office after a fight between Jimmy and his wife. He told Jimmy to put down the bottle, or he would have to shoot him. Jimmy put the bottle down and reached to shake hands, as if the officer was an old friend. The lawman took Jimmy's right hand in his right hand and hit Jimmy with a left hook that knocked him cold as a cucumber. We loaded Jimmy in the back of the patrol car. I didn't see him again for a week, his face was still swollen, and his jaw was wired.

This little episode convinced me to pack up, leave the outfit, and eventually, I wound up bringing my wife and kids back to Okeechobee County and moved into one the of cabins on The River Ranch.

The MacDonald Bull

One of the four Perry brothers that I worked cattle for was Cecil Perry. He had several pastures leased in Polk County. This story is about one area we called the McDonald Place. It was about ten miles south of the town of Groveland.

Two of our Brahma bulls had gotten into a farmer's pasture that adjoined us, and evidently, the farmer didn't want any Brahma calves, so he sent word for us to come and get the two bulls.

We were down there a couple days later working the cattle in our pasture and that afternoon when we got through spraying the cows on our place, we decided to move the two bulls to another place because once they start to roam, the only way to break them is to sell them or move them.

Buddy Fort and I were selected to ride the bulls out of the farmer's pasture and put them on a paved road where they could be pushed between two fences down to a cow pen.

When we got them to the gate to the road, they got suspicious and didn't want to go through the gate. Buddy and I were popping our whips, and one bull went through the gate. The other one bailed off into a cypress swamp. I knew I had to get him because he could go anywhere from there.

I followed him through the cypress swamp to a little clearing about an acre big with one little scrub oak tree in the middle of the opening. When I roped him, he was running wide open, but when he felt the loop on his neck, he ducked behind the oak tree, and my horse Shiloh couldn't stop in time and ran over the slack rope on the ground.

The bull ran around us and basically had me tied in the saddle. When the rope came up under Shiloh's tail, he went airborne. I could feel the rope slacken on me and figured this was my chance to get untangled, and I went straight up with the momentum from the horse's jump. I must have turned over in the air and landed on the back of my head, because I was knocked out cold for a few seconds.

When I sat up, all I could see was Shiloh pulling the bull through the cypress and scrub. They had the trees shaking, and the next thing I heard was barbwire squeaking.

I went out on the road down to where Shiloh and the bull were. Shiloh was facing the bull with the rope tight around its neck and snorting like a freight train. The bull was drawing his last breath. Other than some wire cuts where he had gone through the barbwire, Shiloh was fine.

We got the other bull without a hitch and, to my way of thinking, one out of two wasn't bad!

Brahma Heifers at Lady Lake

While I was working some cattle east of the Ocklawaha River on Highway 42, near a little country store called "Buck and Doe's," a cowman from Lady Lake came to the store and asked Buck to tell me to call him about a job.

In a couple of days, I got hold of the man, and he told me he had some Brahma heifers that he couldn't get out of a 100 acre pasture, and somebody had told him that I had some dogs that would make it so hot on the crazy heifers that they would go anywhere I wanted them to go. I told him that might be a little exaggeration, but if I could bring another cowboy that had a couple of good dogs and, with my two dogs, we would see what could be done.

There were about 120 head of these two year old heifers. The pasture was open with no cross fences. It was located between Lake Griffin and the little town Lady Lake. The cowman wanted to bring some of his crew that was mounted on four wheelers to help. I asked him if that was what he'd been using to drive these cattle with. He admitted they'd been running them for a week and hadn't got one out of the gate yet. I told him we didn't need any help, but, if he wanted to sit in his pickup and watch, that would be fine. "Just don't get out!"

My partner and I arrived and unloaded our horses and dogs. As soon as we rode through the gate, the heifers came over to look us over and then took off to the other end of the pasture. We kept the dogs behind our horses and just followed them kind of slow to get them used to us. They had gotten real curious and were trying to figure out what we had in mind, but I knew what two year old heifers would do if we tried to rush them. They would explode and scatter like quail and go in every direction. But, sooner or later, we had to start the training process and when a little bunch broke off from the herd, it was as good a time as any.

We sent all four dogs to stop the runaways. The dogs downed some of them, and it didn't take them long to pile back into the middle of the herd. Now, they started circling and, every now and then, two or three would break out and make a run for it. The dogs would put them back in the bunch. This was a process that continued over and over until just about every one of them had been nipped by the dogs at least once. There were some ragged ears and bloody noses, but most of the heifers were learning that it was a lot safer to stay in the middle of the bunch. This lasted for at least an hour, and it looked like they were starting to respect the dogs, but the real test would come when we tried to drive them. We had them in a group, but they weren't done testing the dogs yet.

This time it didn't take as long for them to get back in the herd. We started moving them along the line fence and drove them around the whole 100 acres. If we could get them out the gate, there was a lane that was fenced on both sides that went to the pasture that the owner wanted them moved to. We held them tight at the gate, and, finally, a few went through and then some more until there wasn't but about 15 or 20 head that didn't want to go. We got around them, and, when they saw the main bunch going down the lane, they went in and joined them. We followed along behind them for about a half mile until we got to the pasture the cowmen wanted them in.

We shut the gate and rode back to where the owner was still sitting in his pickup. He asked us if it was all right to get out, like we might sic the dogs on him or something. We told him his heifers were where he wanted them. He said he wouldn't have believed it if he hadn't seen it. Two men and four dogs had done in an hour and a half, what six men on four wheelers couldn't do in a week.

I told him, "That's the value of good dogs!"

Cow Dogs

A good cow dog is a sight to behold. Two or three good dogs can handle a bunch of wild cattle that ten men couldn't do anything with. Now you combine a couple of good cowboys and three or four good dogs and you can move a bunch of cattle most anywhere. But there is a method to the madness.

You have to give the dogs the chance to impress the cattle with the fact .... if they run, they are going to pay the price. A rank dog can down a cow in a heartbeat and it only takes a couple of times to get their attention! When you dog break a bunch of cattle, it sticks for a long time. The Florida Cur dog is a classic in selective breeding.

One thing a cowboy cannot do is not brag on his dog.

So the tale gets around that so in so has a good "jip," (a female, usually a young one) and so and so has a good male dog. Even a hundred miles between the cowboys doesn't make a difference. This has been going on for way over a hundred years. The owner of the male dog usually gets the pick of the litter. Some cowboys think the runt will be the best prospect, but not very often. Another way is when the litter is weaned; if there are one or two pups that stand up and growl at you that is a good sign. But, until you get them around a bunch of cows, you don't know what you've got. Usually, through, if you pick the parents, you probably won't be disappointed.

There are some cowboys that are natural "dog men" and some that don't have a clue. I was fortunate to know a couple of them. Theo Johns was one of the best. He could send one dog and hold two, he could send two and hold one, or he could send them all. If you were in high brush and the dogs couldn't see the cows, they would run out a couple hundred feet and stop and look back at Theo, who would motion with his hand in the direction of the cattle and the dogs would change direction, until they found the cattle. I had some good dogs, but I never had the handle on them that Theo had.

Early in the Vietnam War, as the U.S. was getting involved, a good friend, Jimmy White of Oxford in Sumter County, had been called up. I guess he was in the Army Reserve. Well anyway, he had a big brindle cur dog that was from a famous line of catch dogs over at Umatilla in Lake County. The dog's name was "Jake;" Jimmy asked me if I'd take care of him while he was deployed in Asia.

Well, Jake fit right in with my dogs, but he was so rank, I could only use him on special occasions when there was a bad cow or bull that had to be caught. Most of the cowmen that I worked for knew Jimmy White and had heard of Jake and didn't want me to bring him unless they had a cow they hated.

Cecil Perry and his partner in Polk County had such a cow, but they only wanted a mild dose of vengeance because they knew what the "Full Jake" treatment was and wanted me to put my muzzle on him. I didn't like the idea of the dog having a handicap, I was afraid Jake would get hurt. I shouldn't have worried!

When we got the cows bunched, the old cow that was being targeted took off for the scrub like she always did and Jake took off after her, muzzle and all. When he got up next to her head, he made a try for her ear but the muzzle kept him from getting a hold and his made the dog furious. The next thing he did was classic Jake. He ran full speed and hit the crook of her neck and knocked her flat on her side. I roped her and pulled Jake off. We loaded the cow in a horse trailer and they took her to the Webster cow sale.

A couple weeks later I was using Jake in a swamp where the owner of the cattle only wanted them caught and wasn't worried about any collateral damage. Well, we got the job done but in the process Jake got his left front leg broke and I had the vet in Ocala put a cast on it. The vet told me to keep him quiet and let it heal.

Not long after the leg got broke, I had Jake in my dog pen behind my house. My property joined a pasture that belonged to the Double F Ranch. That day we had to gather the cattle there. When I had to leave Jake in the dog pen and ride off with the other dogs, it was killing his soul and he was having a fit. Well, we had the cows bunched and had started to the gate to the main cow pen when all a sudden here comes Jake on three legs, broke leg swinging in a circle. He made a beeline to the first cow he came to and caught her up side of her head. I had to rope Jake and put him up on my horse and haul him home. We had enough help to go on and pen the cows.

I had to take Jake back to the vet and put the cast back on. The vet kept him until it healed and before long Jake was back to his old self. There is a lot more to this dog tale, but that's for later!

Buck Fever

If you've never had it, you don't know what I'm talking about, but if you're a deer hunter and say you never had it you're probably lying.

I had buck fever when I was 15 years old. It happened on my first buck. My Dad and my 10-year-old brother and me were on a little ride in the woods not far from where we lived on Lake Okeechobee. We had my Dad's rifle with us. My Dad and the rifle were like the American Express, he never left home without it!

We hadn't gone very far when my Dad spotted a buck in the sawgrass and reached for his rifle. I started in on him to let me shoot the buck. There was an old fence line along the trail we were driving down. He told me to take a rest on one of the posts and shoot him in the top of his shoulder. The deer was busy feeding in the high grass and hadn't seen or smelt us yet!

By the time I got my rifle on the post, I was shaking so bad, I think the deer heard the post rattling and he raised his head up and looked straight at me. I cut loose with that old 300 Savage; which just about knocked me down. The deer jumped straight up in the air and swapped ends. He's looking around like nothing happened. My Dad told me to drawn down a little, and shoot him again. I quickly composed myself and shot a little lower. This time he went down in a big pile!

I ran out to where he was on the ground. While I was admiring him, I heard a noise about 10 feet past that first deer. There was another dead 8 point laying just beyond that one!

Well, we had two 8 point bucks, and the only way we could figure out how it happened in just two shots, the second buck was looking over the first buck's shoulder and the shot was a little high and hit him between the eyes. Well, after this episode, I was feeling a little cocky, and acting like Davy Crockett around the kids on the ridge of Lake Okeechobee!

But Mother Nature has a way of bringing you back to earth, and the very next trip she did it good. My Dad had a reputation as a extra good deer hunter, and I think he thought the old rifle had more to do with my luck than I did. So, on a trip a year later, he told me I'd be shooting a shotgun, Old Betsy.

On the first morning of deer season, in the year of 1947, I had hid in a palmetto patch on the edge of an open prairie in an area called Hungry Land Slough. I wasn't there thirty-five or forty minutes when I saw a nice buck coming right towards me.

By the time he was close enough to shoot, I had come down with the Mother of all cases of buck fever. I had the palmettos shaking so bad I know he heard me! I tried to settle down, and finally raised up on my knees and aimed and pulled the trigger. Nothing happened. He stopped and looked at me. I pulled the trigger so hard it hurt my finger. By this time, the deer was getting tired of waiting and took off. I looked down and saw the safety was on!

I was planning on keeping this between me and the old 12 gauge; until my Daddy said, "How in the hell did you get my trigger bent on Old Betsy here? Adrenaline does strange things to a kid with a bad case of "buck fever".

Cow Horses

There's never been a horse that couldn't be rode, there's never been a cowboy, that couldn't be throwed!

Next to his wife and kids, the most important and most talked about things in a cowboy's life is his horses. In the thirty-five years that I worked cattle and the twenty-five counties in Florida that I worked them in, I had some good ones.

The first horse that really impressed me wasn't mine, but belonged to a ranch at Twenty Mile Bend called the Consolidated Naval Stores. The foreman of this ranch put me on a big grey gelding called. "Old Blue".

He was an outstanding cow horse and a standard that I would measure all the rest of the horses against for the rest of my career as a cowboy!

The half dozen horses that I rode in the next few years didn't come up to Blue, until I bought the black gelding, that had been abandoned in Okeechobee City. The horse had been shipped by train to a big Cattleman in the area. The Cattleman had died while the horse was en-route. I wound up with the horse, and he was in a league all his own. The first Texas horse I ever owned. His name was Smokey. You could do anything that could be done off a horse while working cattle with him.

One other time, on a trip to the Gainesville Livestock Market with a load of cows, I got to talking to a cowboy friend about horses. He told me about a four year old gelding that was for sale; the horse was the last colt from a stud that was twenty-four years old and was one of the old quarter-horse type of working cow-horses.

The colt's sire was "King Bailey" and his breeding was perfect for a using cow pony. The four year old horse was in Cocoa on the east coast, and belonged to A. Duda and Sons. I bought him for four hundred dollars. His name was Shiloh, and was one of the smartest horses I ever rode. Most ranches that worked "Day-working" cowboys, that were considered good horseman, were often stuck with the dual job of riding one of the outfits' green broke prospects. One cowman that I worked for was good at this. He always had a new outlaw horse that he was afraid of himself, and when we finished working cattle one day, he brought out a big stout gelding that he wanted me to take home and train for a week. He expected me to bring him back next week and work cattle off of him. I was a little leery of this big horse. Otis told me he was a "four year old" "No way!" I said.

Otis started counting on his fingers, "Well maybe six at the outside!" he said. I tied old Red to the cow pen fence and threw a saddle blanket on his back. Well, he froze. I put my saddle on him and pulled the girth up tight. He reared up and broke the rope to his halter and fell over backwards.

Then, he jumped up and took off to the far end of the horse pasture, bucking and raising hell in general. I told Otis I would be back in a couple of days to get what was left of my saddle!

When I arrived two days later "Old Red" was still in the pasture and covered with dried sweat and dirty grass. The saddle was under his belly, upside down, and one of his hind hoofs was through a stirrup. He was hobbling along and when I walked up to him, he put his head in my hand as if to say "Can you help me?" I took the saddle off, the blanket was long gone ... I threw it on his back, he didn't even flinch this time.

I got aboard and walked him up to the cow-pen and loaded him in my horse trailer and worked him in my corral at home for a couple of weeks. It wasn't long before we were working cattle off of him. Leaving him in the pasture hung up with the saddle seemed to be short cut in the training process, but I wouldn't recommend it, unless you had some spare saddles!

Two Weeks at Rattlesnake Island

Back when I was 17 years old, the world was a different place. I was living on Lake Okeechobee and it was a week before Christmas in 1949. Two of my hunting and fishing buddies, Olis Weaver and Gene Williams, myself, and Gene's father, called Doc, were putting together a camping trip to an area called Hungryland Slough. It was located west of Palm Beach and north of a little settlement called Loxahatchee. We planned to camp on a little hammock called Rattlesnake Island.

We had talked my father into taking us to this place that was a good 20 miles straight into the flatwoods. He was to return the day after Christmas – one week later. We had rations enough and, hopefully, could live off the game in the area and be fat and happy when he came to get us.

My dad had a four-wheel drive Jeep pickup truck we had loaded to the brim with provisions. Gene Williams father, Doc, was an excellent camp cook and had a Dutch oven and a little Coleman stove that worked well off of white gas. We also had an old five-man Army squad tent to stay in at night. We made the trip to

Rattlesnake Island without any mishaps.

The Jeep crossed the many creeks and bog holes which only had a little water in them/ We got to the island about sundown. Well, we were having a marvelous time. Big campfire at night, plenty of groceries and on the second day at about sundown I had found some ducks coming in to roost in a little pond and I shot a half-dozen of them. We cleaned and cut them up and cooked them in Doc's Dutch oven. About 10 o'clock that night we were feasting on them. A couple of days went by without any more game, but we had eggs and milk in a cooler. The ice was gone but the stuff was still cool enough and we had plenty of grits and flour, but we needed meat. The salt bacon was still plentiful, but we were getting a little tired of that. We still figured we could make it to the day after Christmas when my dad was to get us.

On Christmas Eve it began to rain. I mean a "toad frog strangler" and an old time "lighter knot floater." It rained all day Christmas and turned cold! The whole country was flooded and our tent had a foot of water in it. We managed to make a little dike around the tent and with everybody dipping with a cooking pot we got most of the water out. We piled palmetto fans as high as we could and bedded down on them and tried to sleep. During the night, a couple of hours before daylight, we heard Doc say in a low voice, "Somebody get a flashlight and be real quiet, I have a "pardner " in bed with me. Bring a rifle, not a shotgun."

I eased over to him with my rifle and flashlight and saw a big rattler "snugged" up next to him. The snake was warm and cozy. I pushed the end of the barrel tight against the snake's head and pulled the trigger. What happened next was a sight to behold.

Although the snake's head was blown off, the snake came up and wrapped around Doc! The snake was dead, but Doc didn't know it and he proceeded to knock the tent down trying to find the door out.

A couple of days later the food situation was getting serious. We had the stuff to cook with, but had run out of stuff to cook! On the morning of the fifth day after Christmas, we heard some Sandhill Cranes whooping in the direction of the marsh that laid to the south of us. I decided to try and slip up on them. The Sandhill Crane has almost as much meat as a turkey. I was carrying my dad's 300 Savage rifle and when I got on the edge of the marsh, I could see five or six whooping cranes a couple of hundred yards away. There was just enough cover for me to crawl into gunshot range. I picked one out and knocked him down. I tried a second shot but they were in the air and I missed. Well, we were happy campers and had a major feed time that night.

The next morning abut 10 o'clock we heard the Jeep coming through the flatwoods. The water had gone down enough that my dad could work his way to us. He told us he had tried to get to us a couple of days after the storm. He had bogged down about halfway and had to walk out to the Palm Beach Highway and catch a ride back to the farm.

He was finally able to get a tractor to the Jeep and pull it out of the bog he had got in nearly a week before. He told the tractor driver to wait and follow us to the highway. We loaded our gear in record time and said "good-bye" to Rattlesnake Island!

Wild Hogs

When I was 17 years old and living on the ridge of Lake Okeechobee, my father came home one Saturday night and told my mother he had finally won big at poker.

One of my dad's passions was playing poker with some of his local farmer friends. It was a casual game where they talked shop and crops, and my dad was a notoriously unlucky poker player. The stakes were always small, and it never hurt much. But, this Saturday night was different.

My dad was all excited as he told my mother about the game. My mother was getting flustered because she didn't approve of gambling of any kind, but, if it was a substantial win, she might join in on the windfall because there were always things we could use - groceries, being one of them. "Well, let's see the money," she said, finally getting in the mood.

My brother, Jerry, and I were supposed to be in bed, but we were light sleepers, and we always expected a fight on Saturday night after a poker game.

We jumped out of bed and came into the kitchen. "What money?" we both asked at the same time. My dad dropped his head a little and said the winnings weren't actually in cash, but were worth a lot of money.

He explained that one of the card players was a man name Comer, who was a well-to-do blacksmith in Pahokee. Comer owned a bunch of wild hogs in a place called Big Mound, south of Indiantown.

Back in the 40s and 50s, wild hogs were property just like cattle. You marked the hog's ears with your personal mark, which was registered in the local courthouse.

In this case, it was Palm Beach County. My dad had won two marks from Comer, who said there were hundreds of hogs around the area south of Big Mound.

Well, my mother was always the practical one in the family and, much to our surprise, said, "What the hell are we going to do with a bunch of wild hogs?" We knew she was upset. We had never before heard her cuss. Still, daddy told her we were going to catch them.

My mind was racing, and I piped up. "I'll catch them for you, daddy." My 12-year-old brother added, "I'll help, too,"

At the time, my dad was busy farming, but the hogs were on his mind, and the next weekend he planned on making a trip to Big Mound to survey the situation. He told me I could go, but my brother had to stay with our mother.

It wasn't just around the corner. We started early. My dad had a 4-wheel drive Jeep pickup, and we went north toward Indiantown to an old trail that was barely a road running south through the piney woods for about 10 miles.

First, we came to Comer's camp house and about a half mile farther was a big Indian mound. Next, was an orange grove with an old tin shack where the Everglades started.

We saw a lot of hog signs on this trip, some turkey and a couple of deer. We decided the old tin shack, shaded with mango trees, would make a good headquarters for our operation.

Comer told us that most of the hogs were in the marsh, it being the dry season, and all. So, my dad approached the area from the Palm Beach Canal. The hogs were in the area feeding on pink root, a nutritious tuber that kept the hogs in fine shape.

The next weekend, we took a boat up the canal, called the 9 Mile Canal. We had brought some dogs my dad had bought at Okeechobee City that were guaranteed "hog dogs."

At the end of the canal was a mound with a rubber tree on it that made a good campsite. We got there at sundown and put up a tent. There were three of us: me, dad, and my Uncle Manning.

We ate a cold supper and bedded down. The dogs were outside the tent, and at about 2 a.m. a panther cut loose with a blood-curdling scream. The "bad" dogs tore the tent down getting in, and the next morning we couldn't get them off the mound. They kept whining and looking over their shoulders. We could see, right away, they didn't have what it took to handle a bad hog.

In the meantime, I had a good hunting buddy by the name of Olis Weaver who told me that if we could convince my dad to let us catch the hogs, he could get a swamp buggy from a man over at West Palm Beach, and we could find our own dogs to catch hogs.

I started in on my dad with this proposition. "Son," he said," what you're talking about is a lot more dangerous than you think. Those hogs will cut you and your dogs to ribbons."

"Daddy, we won't take any chances. We'll shoot the hogs as soon as the dogs bay them up." We can dress them at the camp at Big Mound and bring the meat back home in an ice chest and sell it."

This was true because for a long time after WWII meat was scarce and in demand by the farm help all around the lake. Well, we started making sense to dad, but mother was a different story.

"You'll get yourself killed is what will happen," she said.

The farm my dad managed had 50 to 100 men working it, and, depending on the season, he knew he could sell every piece of pork we could have brought home. Besides, he got the farmhands' money before they did, and collecting was not a problem.

"Well, let's see if you can get the right dogs, and then we'll give it a try," he said. "But I'm going with you to start with."

Getting the right dogs turned out to be our main problem. Everybody in the area with an old cur dog was willing to contribute. We had a couple tame hogs in a pen that we would show to the new prospects, and everyone that looked at the hogs would run back to the truck and jump in the cab. I bet we run through a dozen sorry dogs. Finally, I heard of a cowboy, John Holt, in Indiantown who had a sure-enough hog dog. The dog was a 90 pound Florida yellow cur. John was having trouble with him going out at night and catching hogs on his own. John wanted a cow dog, not a hog dog, and so he sold him to us, the dog named Ring. We also got a 40 pound bulldog and a Walker hound that was a natural trail dog. Finally, we were in business.

One weekend, with my dad along, we camped at the old shed at Big Mound. The rainy season had started a month earlier, and the water had run the hogs up into the piney woods. It was about 9 a.m., Saturday morning, and Weaver and I were going to take the dogs on a little round behind the camp. My dad had loaned me his 300 Savage rifle, and Weaver was carrying a 9mm Mauser. We hadn't gone 200 yards from camp when the dogs took off, baying up into a thicket next to the big mound.

There was a growling, squealing fight going on, and, when we caught up to the commotion, we saw a little boar weighing about 90 pounds. The bulldog had one of its ears, and Ring had the other. We got him down, marked his ears, and set him loose until we were ready for him. We put leads on the dogs and had to drag them back to camp.

When we got back, dad said we'd better check the dogs for cuts. Sure enough, the bulldog, whom Weaver had named Buck, had a gash under his chin, close to his jugular, Ring was cut in his stomach. The Walker didn't have a scratch on him. Dad said we'd better get some waxed thread and a big needle to sew up the cuts. This made a big impression on us. Those dogs were hard to find, and we couldn't afford for them to get killed.

We got the idea to use a leather smith in Pahokee, good with shoes and boots, to make some protective outfits for our dogs, especially for the bulldog who would "catch."

The leather smith made a vest for Buck that went from his neck to his haunches and laced up the back, like a boot. Mostly, we had to carry Buck to the fight, but the vest worked like a charm. The other two dogs were protected by wide leather collars and a flap that covered some of their chests, which gave them the freedom to maneuver.

The next weekend was to be a meat trip, and dad took us to Big Mound and we camped in the shack. The next morning, Weaver and I and the dogs headed east along the marsh next to the piney woods. Buck, following alongside us, was getting used to his vest. Just then, the Walker hound sniffed the air and took off like a shot, Ring right behind him. Soon, they bayed up in a palmetto patch, cornering two sows and a boar.

We killed the boar and one sow as soon as possible, the other had to be wrestled by the back legs away from Buck, who had a death grip on the sow's ear. I put my gun next to the ear and shot the sow and we still had to pry Buck loose. We loaded the hogs onto the swamp buggy, headed back to camp, and skinned the hogs and put the meat on ice.

This was a trial run to see if we had a marketable product. The pork went like hot cakes at a local sawmill. We almost had a riot. Weaver made a deal on the use of the swamp buggy, which was necessary to get us into the marsh where the pink root was. We caught 49 hogs that year and marked a bunch of pigs.

Old General

My grandfather, Bill Roberts (who I got my name from) could be considered a pioneer Florida Cracker. He was born in the "Big Scrub" many years before it officially became the Ocala National Forest.

The local settlers were always having problems with predators in those days. The predators, panthers and bears, were after the hogs and chickens; and the bears even killed calves, and, occasionally, a grown cow.

When this happened in the settlements, it meant a posse of sorts. But sometimes the people decided to go big game hunting with no other reason than to exercise the hounds, and, in the case of bears, for the meat.

One time in particular that my father, Phil Roberts, told me about was just a regular bear hunt. The thing that made it unusual was Grandfather had planned on making it a training experience for a big, white English Bulldog by the name of "General." The dog had become an aggravation in his old age. He was terrorizing the tame hogs in the community. Grandfather figured he would take General on a bear hunt and maybe it would change his attitude.

Well, the hunters had jumped a big male bear and Grandpa was getting close to where the bear was bayed up in a big palmetto patch. Grandpa was driving a wagon and General was sitting on the bench seat next to him. They were having trouble getting the wagon up close because the mule didn't like the situation either, but General was having a fit to get in the palmettos - it was his first bear hunt.

When Grandpa got as close as he was going to get, he told General to "get 'em." General piled off the seat almost on top of the bear. There was a terrible yelp and General came out over the palmettos in a rotating spin and landed about 15 feet from the wagon. In 3 or 4 jumps, General was on the seat next to Grandpa. When he said, "Get 'em General!' again, the dog started twisting on the seat and whining but nothing was going to get him back in that palmetto thicket again. This seemed to cure the dog of terrorizing the tame hog population anymore.

Buster and the Alligator

y the late 70's, I had moved from the four acres next to the Double F Ranch. I had sold my house and gone to help my father and mother who were getting ready to retire. I bought a house on a rock road called Panther Road, where my father had a pond that he had been putting bass and bream in for several years.

On a trip through the forest one time, my father picked up a five foot gator that had been hit by a car. The gator wasn't hurt real bad, and my dad put him in the pond on Panther Road. With all the fish and turtles in the pond, the gator, in a couple years, was a healthy seven footer. For some reason, my father named the gator "Jerry." My brother was also named Jerry, and I never could figure that out - my brother and the alligator didn't have that much in common.

At this time, my father would make the rounds every morning through the forest and pick up road kill to feed Jerry - the gator, not my brother! By the time I moved to Panther Road, the gator was at least nine feet long and probably weighted at least 1,000 pounds from all the food my dad was feeding him.

I had one cow dog that I brought with me to Panther Road. It was old Buster and the highlight of his day was to go in the fenced-in area with my dad to feed the gator. He'd stand at the top of a big mound of dirt and bark his head off. This was getting a little annoying to everybody, including the gator, but Buster wasn't stupid, and he kept about 20 feet between him and the gator.

One day after about 30 minutes of constant barking, I decided to wean Buster of this aggravating habit. I had a cane fishing pole about 15 feet long and I slipped up behind the dog, who had all his attention on the gator, and I goosed him in the rear with the pole. He went airborne, and was headed down towards the gator. While he was in the air, he had already put his legs in reverse, and, when he landed about six feet from the gator, the dirt was already flying, and Buster had wound up back on top of the mound of dirt.

Well, this had him shut up for a couple days. But, when he started up again, all I had to do was show him the cane pole!

The Barker Gang Shoot Out
at Ocklawaha, Florida

The Barker Gang Shoot Out at Ocklawaha, Florida in 1935, has been told and re-told, and been on T.V. several times. But, I know a story from a man that I used to work cattle for that was there and witnessed the whole thing.

When I heard the story from him, it was 25 years after the fact. This is what the cowman told me.

Back in the early 30s, his uncle had a contract from the county to haul the school kids from the Summerfield area to the Belleview School. Somehow, a rumor was going on around the area that something big was going to happen in Ocklawaha that morning. As the owner of the contract bus picking up the kids early that morning, it was decided unanimously that they would detour to Ocklawaha to see what the deal was all about! They got there about the time the shooting started.

The FBI and the local law had surrounded a two story house on Lake Weir on the tip that the Barker gang of bank robbers and cold blood killers were residing in the house. When shots were fired from the house, the law and FBI agents started pouring machine and shot gun blasts at the outlaws inside. Thirty-five hundred rounds was exchanged before the gang inside stopped shooting. It turned out to be only Maw and son Fred, and they were both stone cold dead!

Over the next few years, the rest of the gang was killed or captured. Every so often, the sleepy, little village of Ocklawaha is lit up again with the rattle of gunfire (fire crackers) from a reenactment of the shoot out, and Maw and Fred are killed again!